LINGUISTIC SITUATION IN NORTH-EAST INDIA

About the Author

Professor Mrinal Miri is an outstanding scholar of the country. He is a former Director of Indian Institute of Advanced Study, Shimla and a former President of North East India Council for Social Science Research, Shillong. At present he is the Vice-Chancellor of North Eastern Hill University, Shillong.

LINGUISTIC SITUATION IN NORTH-EAST INDIA

Edited by

Mrinal Miri

Published for
NORTH-EAST INDIA COUNCIL
FOR
SOCIAL SCIENCE RESEARCH
by

CONCEPT PUBLISHING COMPANY, NEW DELHI - 110059

ISBN 81-8069-026-1

First Edition, 1982
Second Edition, 2003

Published and Printed by

Ashok Kumar Mittal
Concept Publishing Company
A/15-16, Commercial Block, Mohan Garden,
NEW DELHI-110059 (India)

Phones : 2[illegible]1460, 25351794
Fax : 091-1[illegible] 25357103
E-mail : publishing@conceptpub.com

PREFACE TO THE SECOND EDITION

The first edition of this book was published in 1982. Two decades have passed since then. The basic issues however of linguistic scenario of North East India have not changed much. We need to understand the problems of relationship between language, culture and politics.

We would like to thank Concept Publishing Company and Mr. Ashok Kumar Mittal for taking initiative to bring out the second edition of the book.

7th October, 2002

B. DATTA RAY

Secretary

N.E.I.C.S.S.R

PREFACE TO THE FIRST EDITION

North-East India Council for Social Science Research in association with the Department of Sociology and Anthropology, North Eastern Hill University held on September 25-26, 1979 a seminar on the Linguistic Situation in North East India in its effort to study the multi-dimensional issues involved in the development process of North East India. The special focus of the seminar was on the linguistic situation with particular reference to the problems of inter-ethnic communication, linguistic identity and growth of ethnic consciousness on the basis of linguistic affiliation in post-independence period. The attitude of the numerous ethnic groups in the maintenance and shift from various languages spoken was brought to light in the seminar. Attempts were made on the basis of phonological and syntactical study of the language to arrive at deeper understanding of the underlying historical and cultural identity of the people of the region.

We were much encouraged in our study by the wide response from scholars from different regions. We are grateful to Dr. A. K. Dhan, the then Vice-Chancellor, North Eastern Hill University for agreeing to inaugurate the seminar. We are also grateful to Rev. Brother M. G. Shannon, Principal, St. Edmund's College, Anthropological Survey of India, Central Institute of Indian Languages, Mysore, and the Chief Regional Manager, State Bank of India, Shillong, for their support in making this study possible.

Dr. Mrinal Miri, a past president of NEICSSR has kindly edited the papers for publication. We thank him for it. We thank also Mr. Sarkar and Ri Khasi Press, Shillong for undertaking the printing of this book.

9th August, 1982

B. DATTA RAY
Secretary
N.E.I.C.S.S.R

CONTENTS

Preface to the Second Edition 5
Preface to the First Edition 7
Introduction by ***Mrinal Miri*** 11

PART – I
LANGUAGE AND POLITICS

1. Language in Politics in North-East India: The Background 21
   — *Amalendu Guha*
2. Khasi-Bengali to Roman : The Colonial Transformation of the Khasi-Jaintia Hills 26
   — *Shyamadas Bhattacharya* and *Jayanta Bhusan Bhattacharjee*
3. Evolution of Assamese as a Medium of Instruction 49
   — *M. Kar*
4. The Coming of the Alphabet : A Study of the Scripts of Some North-Eastern Languages 69
   — *P.K. Bandyopadhyay*
5. Trend of the Language and Culture of Manipur 76
   — *E. Nilakanta Singh*
6. Language Problem in the North-East Region 83
   — *B.N. Talukdar*

PART – II
LANGUAGE, CULTURE AND SOCIETY

7. Kinship and Language : An Exploration of Sapir-Whorf Hypothesis in the Garo Language 89
   — *D.N. Majumdar*
8. Non-Standard Forms of Assamese : Their Socio-cultural Role 101
   — *Birendranath Datta*

9. Loan Words in North-Eastern India 111
— *P. Goswami*
10. Sociology of Language : North-Eastern Case 117
— *Sudhansu S. Tunga*
11. Khasi Language and the Changing Society 125
— *Jeep Sandy Khonglah* and *A.P. Sinha*
12. Sino-Tibetan Languages of North-East India : Social Aspects 130
— *P.C. Bhattacherji*
13. A Short Note on Mising Phonology 134
— *Tabu Taid*
14. A Few Aspects of some of the Languages of Arunachal Pradesh 145
— *K. Das Gupta*

Index 153

INTRODUCTION

One of the difficulties of editing the proceedings of a seminar is that of organizing the material in such a manner as to give it a sense—even if it is a vague of coherence and purpose. In spite of the best efforts on the part of the organizers to formulate a seminar problem in relatively definite terms with more or less clear bounds, the papers that eventually come up for discussion fail, nearly always, to remain within the confines of these limits. The volume that results is thus frequently no more than a collection of unconnected papers.The problem is further exacerbated by the fact that very often detailed records of discussions held are also not available.

The present volume, as the reader will quickly realize, suffers somewhat from this difficulty. However, what makes it still worth publishing is that in the general state of ignorance about the North-East, this volume at least brings to light the enormity of the phenomenon of language in this part of the country. And some of the papers deal with their problems with vigour and incisiveness, while others contain valuable information. Still others are almost the very first attempts at systematic understanding of a certain kind.

It seems to me that a question which we cannot and *must not* avoid asking in a fundamental way is: "What ought to be my attitude to another's language?" I think of it primarily as a moral question capable of a rational answer; and although much of our talk about the problems of language in this country presumes some answer to this question, we have really not faced the question with the kind of intellectual explicitness and honesty that it deserves.

This is not the place for me to discuss this question in any detail. I would, however, like to consider some of the grounds on which we might normally appreciate or criticise another's language. One might say any of the following in criticism of a language:

(i) that it is a distorted version of another language (e.g. "Assamese is a distortion of Bengali"); (ii) that it does not have a script; (iii) that it does not have a literature ("the Mishing language does not have a literature and, therefore, it is only a 'dialect' "), (iv) that it is incomplete (inadequate) ("the Bengali language says much better what the Apatani language can say only inadequately").

To take these in order: (i) Two languages may be very closely similar to one another, and can be shown even to have a common origin but this does not make either of them an inferior version of the other or of the "original" language. A language—or, to use Wittgenstein's phrase, a "form of life"—is what it is and not another one in a different guise. "The individuation of a language is undoubtedly a difficult task, and often in the actual act of individuation, considerations other than linguistic (in the broad sense in which a language encompasses a distinct form of life)"[1] may be involved. Such considerations may be political, economic, historical and racial and so on; or, of course, all of them together. But the claim by a group that their native language is autonomous and distinct, although motivated partly by any or all of these considerations—is there ever a pure, unmixed motive of human action?—is almost invariably associated with the perception, by the group, of significant differences in their form of life. To think that this language is a distorted version of one's own may exhibit an arrogance and insensitiveness which could be compared to the arrogance and insensitiveness of thinking that there is no way of looking at a thing other than one's own.

(ii) To criticise another language on the ground that it does not have a script is peculiarly misplaced. The script of a language is not an internal part of it. It stands, as it were, outside the language in a way in which the form of life cannot stand outside the language and it gets whatever "life" it has *from* the language and not the other way round. A script without a language is "*dead*"; but a language without a script is still very much a language, not *less* of

---

1. I have argued elsewhere for the view that a language does encompass a distinct form of life, a distinct culture, if you like.

a one. The presence of a script may undoubtedly help in the growth of a language in so far as it facilitates the exploration of the possibilities of the language, but such exploration can take place, and *have* taken place without the help of a script. The absence of a script is not a criterion of the poverty of a language.

(iii) The third kind of criticism is, however, serious. The possibility of literature is inherent in any language, and it is in literature that the bounds of meaning of a language are continuously explored and extended. A language which has not developed a literature has not, as it were, "realized" itself. But is there in fact a language which does not have a literature? If the emergence of a literature is not thought to be dependent on the existence of a written tradition—and it will be merely silly to think so—then I do not think there is in fact a language without a literature. For, literature will then include stories, songs, legends, "myths" (if that is the correct word), parables, incantations and so on. It is quite safe to say that there is not a language which does not have a good measure of all these. In fact quite frequently, the primary source of creativity even in a written tradition of literature is to be found in the symbols employed in these stories, songs, etc.[2]

(iv) In a sense, no language is complete, because it must be possible for new things to be said in it. But when a language is criticised as being incomplete what is meant is that some things are (can be) said in that language, but vaguely, confusedly and inadequately, while the same things can be said clearly and adequately, in another language. And this is not true. An attempt to "improve" a language by inducting elements into it from a different language so that the "same" things may be said more completely in the former, cannot succeed; because, the result of such an attempt

2. "Language is something that can have a literature. This is where it is so different from chess. And if we include folksongs and stories, then literature is immediately important in almost any language; important for ways in which things said in the language are understood. It has to do with the 'force' which one remarks or another may have in that language, for instance. And in this way, it has to do also what is seen to make sense and what is not." Rush Rhees, *Discussions of Wittgenstein*, London, 1970.

is not that the same things are said less confusedly in the language, but that something different is also said in the language now. When Wittgenstein says that any given language is "complete" he means that you fall into a confusion if you try to provide a more ample and more perfect system for what may be said in it. Whatever may be said in your new system, it will not be what was said in the original "language game".

I believe that a language affords a specially intimate and the most authentic access to the culture of the people whose native language it is. A culture, of course, includes things like the way people cultivate their lands, bury their dead, celebrate marriages, build their houses and so on; and a study of the culture must include all these and more. But these people's language (which, of course, includes its literature) is not another of these cultural things that they have. It embodies, as it were, the special "life" and tone of the entire culture. That is why mastering another's language is not just a matter of mastering its grammatical rules, vocabulary and accent. It is much more importantly a matter of understanding nuances of gestures, pauses, voice and subtle differences of action and reaction. In the absence of such an understanding, to speak another's language with a mastery over its grammar is speaking it without grasping the life of the language. And one's access to another culture based on what might be called a mere "mechanical" understanding of its language (its grammar and pronunciation) is therefore bound to be superficial. Also, therefore, any *assessment* of the culture based on such an understanding of its language must be fraught with danger—both intellectual and moral. There will be a great danger of assimilating it to one's own and applying to it one's own criteria of evaluation. If the assimilation is wrong the evaluation is bound to be wrong. Someone who thinks of polyandry as practised in some societies as indicating an extraordinary moral depravity in the women of these societies, makes this type of mistake of assimilation and evaluation.

In the following passage from his *Celebration of Awareness*, Ivan Illich speaks of silences, but his argument can be extended to encompass a great variety of other things. I quote it because it says with such tremendous eloquence and with such telling effect what ideally I would like to have been able to say. Thus to quote Illich:

> To learn a language in a human and mature way, therefore, is to accept the responsibility for its silences and for its sounds. The gift a people gives us in teaching us their language is more a gift of the rhythm, the mode and subtleties of its system of silences than of its system of sounds. It is an intimate gift for which we are accountable to the people who have entrusted us with their tongue. A language of which I know only the words and not the pauses is a continuous offence.
>
> It takes more time and effort and delicacy to learn the silence of a people than to learn its sounds. Some people have a special gift for this. Perhaps this explains why some missionaries, notwithstanding their efforts, never come to speak properly, communicate delicately through silences. Although they speak with the "accent of natives" they remain forever thousands of miles away. The learning of the grammar of silence is an art much more difficult to learn than the grammar of sounds.
>
> As words must be learned by listening and by painful attempts at imitation of a native speaker, so silences must be acquired through delicate openness to them. Silence has its pauses and hesitations, its rhythms and expressions and inflections; its durations and pitches, and times to be and time not to be. Just as with our words there is an analogy between our silence with men and with God. To learn the full meaning of one, we must practice and deepen the other. (Illich, 1970).

2. From what I have said, it will be obvious to the reader of the volume that I differ substantially, in spirit at least, with some of the contributors. I should particularly like to record here my difference with the views of Sudhansu S. Tunga. Quite apart from the material presented in his paper, "Sociology of Language: North-Eastern Case", I find its tone wholly objectionable.

Amalendu Guha ("Language Politics in North-Eastern India") with characteristic lucidity discuss the rise of "little nationalism" in the North-East and the role that language has played in this development. However, as he points out, in the hills region of the area "a pool of other symbols like common dress, diet, economic ways and folk culture rather than language as such, has been the primary rallying point for nationality formation".

In their substantial paper, "Khasi-Bengali to Roman: the Colonial Transformation of the Khasi-Jaintia Hills", Shyamdas Bhattacharya and Jayanta Bhusan Bhattacharjee trace, with clarity and insight, the changes of fortune of the Bengali language and script in the Khasi and Jaintia Hills under the impact of British colonialism.

M. Kar describes with great care the "evolution of Assamese as a medium of instruction" during the colonial period; he also sees the origin of the language problem, which has figured so prominently in the politics of Assam in recent decades, in the wranglings about the medium of instruction in the District of Goalpara during the nineteen twenties and thirties.

In his paper, "trend of the Language and Culture of Manipur", E. Nilakanta Singh presents the stark reality of Manipur in simple but telling language. The problem of diversity in this tiny state is overwhelming, and the future seems bleak.

B. N. Talukdar makes a fervent plea for the depoliticization of the admittedly complex language problem of the region.

The kinship terminology of the Garo language is fascinating and in his equally fascinating paper, "Kinship and Language: An Exploration of Sapir-Whorf Hypothesis in the Garo Language", D. N. Majumdar analyses the organic relationship between this terminology and what he calls Garo "culture" (as distinct from "society", "environment" and "psychology"). I am not sure about this last distinction, but the paper remains an important contribution to cultural linguistics.

Birendranath Datta's paper is a sensitive survey of the amazing variety of "non standard" forms of Assamese spoken in Assam and some of the neighbouring areas. These vary, as he shows, not only according to region, but, within the same region, according to community, class and religion.

Promod Chandra Bhattacharji's papers makes a useful survey of the speakers of the Sino-Tibetan group of language in the region.

P. Goswami's excellent paper on loan words in Assam and

some other languages of the region shows how enormously profitable this kind of study can be in understanding social changes and intercultural relationships.

Tabu Taid's paper is a pioneering work on Mising phonology and K. Das Gupta's paper brings out interesting features of the language spoken in Arunachal Pradesh.

It remains for me to thank the North-East India Council for Social Science Research, which has done such wonderful work in the field of social research in the area over the past decade, for asking me to edit this volume. This organization, under the extremely able and creative guidance of its Secretary, Dr. B. Datta-Ray, has done more perhaps than any other comparable organization to promote academic awareness of the societies of the North-Eastern part of our country. It has been my privilege to be associated with its work.

MRINAL MIRI

PART – I

LANGUAGE AND POLITICS

1

LANGUAGE IN POLITICS IN NORTH-EAST INDIA
The Background

Amalendu Guha

I

Language politics stem from objectively distinct ethnic groups' aspirations for achieving certain rights—those ranging from the recognition of their group identities in the matter of language and culture in some form or other within the Indian Union to the right of forming a separate, sovereign state outside it.

There could be two approaches to understanding the language situation in its political aspects. One, the conventional national integration approach from above: and the other, the nationality-formation approach from below.[1]

The first approach starts with the assumption that India is a nation-state, representing in all-inclusive terms diverse linguistic and other ethnic groups which are either already fully integrated or are still in the process of being integrated. Here, the emphasis is on assimilation. What is brought into focus is a pan-Indian identity, a composite nationalism, to which minority ethnic groups, if lacking integration and loyalty, are to be assimilated.

The second approach starts with the given multi-ethnic situation, takes note of the process of nationality-formation within that situation and examines how the emergent nationalities are mutually related within the given state. Here, the emphasis is on the recognition of differentiation, rather than on assimilation. 'One nation, one state' principle is not recognized. In a country like India, the multiple nationalities are said to have their political unity rooted in the shared memories of their common struggle against the British imperialism and in the considerations for convenience and common advantages of sharing a single political structure, and not in the awareness of a common national identity.[2]

Whatever be the approach—the one from above or the other from below—it cannot be denied that the growth of nationalism in India has simultaneously proceeded along two tracks. There are two streams of nationalism. One, at the all-India plane, coextensively with the whole Indian territory and all ethnic groups, demanding loyalty to the Indian nationality. And the other, at the regional-linguistic planes, demanding loyalty to the respective regional nationalities. Elsewhere, I have called the former as great nationalism and the latter as little nationalism—both moreoftenthan not accommodative to each other.[3] These are not necessarily pulls in opposite directions, but have been and are, by and large, complementary to each other. Simultaneously pulls of great and little nationalisms have created, or are in the process of creating, dual national personalities (whether recognized so by the Constitution or not), that is, dualized nationalities within the Indian Union in which no single nationality is dominant[4] Hence, India is better described as a multi-national state rather than as a nation-state.

Ethnic groups may be distinguished from one another by such criteria as language, religion, caste, tribe and, of course, region. However, such distinguishing features do not by themselves, automatically and necessarily, lead to the emergence of national consciousness. It emerges when a rising middle class, belonging to such a group, steps in to mediate. The class highlights one or more of these distinguishing features to make the group self-conscious so that by mobilizing mass support, it could win some class demands, skilfully posed as the group's national demand. Thus being conscious of a community of culture through the mediation of its middle class, the group is slowly transformed into a nationality, attaining or desiring to attain substantial political significance within or outside the existing state.

This is how Indian nationalism and the Bengali, Assamese,

Naga, Mizo and Khasi nationalisms and their likes developed—some early, others late— in course of the last one and a half centuries in our country.

Keeping this broad frame in view, the evolution of little nationalisms in north-east India, involving the language issue as a major symbol of group identity, will be discussed in the remaining part of this chapter.

II

Provincial boundaries in British India were fixed in accordance with considerations of convenience and economy, rather than of regional homogeneities. The province of Assam, therefore, engulfed almost the whole of present north-east India, with its many region-based languages and tribes. With the rise of the middle classes in mainland India during the nineteenth century, there was a simultaneous development of both great and little nationalisms. Until 1917, i.e. before the rise of Gandhiji to national leadership, the Indian National Congress used to champion the cause of great nationalism alone, without taking into consideration India's multi-ethnic and multinational situation. However, alongside of this mainstream of nationalism, there was the other stream—the little nationalisms of the Bengali, Marathi, Assamese and other nationalities. Their middle class wanted for themselves a share of the market as well as of regional political power to ensure it, even as they were together fighting for India's independence from the yoke of British rule.

In north-east India, Bengali and Assamese middle classes came, in that process, into conflict with each other. Their mutual competition for jobs, business and other opportunities, which were limited under the colonial regime, was keen. In course of that competition and conflict, the Assamese middle class plays its role in making its own ethnic group self-conscious about its language and political rights and about the desirability of an autonomous status for the Assamese nationality, in some form or other. The national consciousness in the case of the Assamese fairly developed by 1920.

With the rise of the middle classes amongst the hill tribes thereafter, this process of nationality-formation slowly extended to the hills region as well. There, the Khasi, Garo, Naga and Mizo nationalities emerged, in due course, in their respective regional base by 1947. They too, nurtured their languages with pride and aspired for autonomy in some form or other. This unfolding process continued through the post-independence period which saw a number of regional national movements, the constitutional provision for and extension of the Sixth Schedule and the progressive break-up of the composite province of Assam into a number of autonomous states and regions.

III

Language, as a mobilizing symbol of nationality-formation, has not however played the same role everywhere. Nor is it always of primary importance, (e.g. in Nagaland) in this respect. The point may be illustrated.

In the case of the Assamese nationality-formation, the language symbol remained all along the strongest spiritual bond. Status of the language in offices and educational institutions and relative numerical strength of the Assamese speaking community from census to census— these have remained the chief concerns of Assamese nationalism. This nationalism if often sustained by positing 'Bengali expansionism' as the main obstacle in the way of the development of the Assamese language and culture. Hence, its political programme includes measures that would permanently ensure both numerical and linguistic-cultural domination of the Assamese within the state. At times, Assamese little nationalism becomes fierce and aggressive, so far as the ethnic minorities are concerned.

This model has repeated itself in the case of other little nationalisms of north-east India, only with this difference that language as a mobilizing symbol has played a lesser role and that the Assamese, too, had been suspected of "expansionism". In Mizoram, the Khasi-Jaintia Hills and the Garo Hills, Mizo, Khasi and Garo languages are respectively, the dominant languages but not the only languages. Here, the dominant little nationalisms have stood for assimilation of smaller local (tribal), linguistic groups to the main group. To this extent, languages play a positive role in transcending tribal boundaries and widening the base of the respective nationalities, all of them having well-defined home land regions. In all these cases, attempts at making Assamese the official language in the old state of Assam boomeranged. However, a pool of other symbols like common dress, diet, economic ways and folk culture rather than language as such has been the primary rallying point for nationality-formation in the hills region.

This is evident from the case of Nagaland. There are several Naga languages, all more or less in the same stage of development and none dominant. Here, therefore, of all symbols of identity, language plays the least role. It is the use of Nagamese, an artificial link language, over and above English and the Roman script that helps reduce the communication gap amongst the Naga tribes who together form the Naga nationality. Nagaland is thus an epitome of multi-lingual India.

Finally, despite constitutional arrangements for regional autonomy the problem of national minorities persist even within the autonomous states. The Bengali-speaking, Buddhist Chakma tribe in Mizoram and the Boro-Kachari (and Miri) tribal population in Assam are resisting assimilation as aggrieved national minorities. They do not fit into our analytical frame. All said, the problem of minority rights will continue to persist at all levels of the Indian state structure, even if the aspirations of all the emergent nationalities are largely fulfilled. Drive for economic development is bound to lead to a situation in which peoples of many nationalities will intermingle all over India. Thus, national minorities will be there everywhere.

NOTES AND REFERENCES

1. Paul R. Brass, *Language Religion and Politics in North India* (Delhi, 1974), ch. I. We have found the analytical frame of this book useful with certain modifications.
2. *Ibid.*
3. Amalendu Guha, "Great Nationalism, little nationalism and the problem of integration : tentative view" in *Economic and Political Weekly*, Vol. XIV. Annual Number Feb. 1978.
4. There is similarity with the Yugoslav situation. See Paul Shoup, *Communism and the Yugoslav National Question* (Columbia University Press, 1968)., pp. 262-3.

2

KHASI-BENGALI TO ROMAN
The Colonial Transformation of Khasi-Jaintia Hills

Shyamdas Bhattacharya and
Jayanta Bhusan Bhattacharjee

The impact of Bengali language and Bengali script on the society and economy of the Khasi-Jaintia in the pre-colonial and early colonial periods and the consequence of the colonial change from Bengali to Roman character provide significant fields of research for the social scientists. This chapter is an attempt to focus the dialectical process through which Bengali language and script, first appearing on the fringe of Khasi and Jaintia Hills, gradually percolated into the heart of the free tribal society, and the problem and crises that this process accelerated in the pace of life after it came in confrontation with the colonial pattern of culture planted by the British Raj. It also makes a plea for the thorough linguistic study of the influence upon Khasi of the Indian languages in general and Bengali in particular. A probe into the etymology, phonetics, phonology and semantics of Khasi words and a study of Khasi orthography would explore a wide range of rich materials that the historians might profitably use for reconstruction of the social and economic history of the Khasi-Jaintias, and while doing so, one would have the pleasure of noticing the fact that regional history in spite of local tone and temper is not altogether different from the history of the national mainstream of which it forms a part.

Pre-colonial Khasi-Bengali Relations

The Khasi state like Sohra, Shella, Mawlong and Nongkhlaw extended over some adjoining plain tracts of Sylhet in Bengal and the Bengali speaking ryots were required to visit the hills to pay tribute and homage to their repective *Syiems* and *Darbars*.[1] Similarly, the southern portion of the Jaintia (Jayantis) kingdom comprised of the very fertile tract of level land extending from the foot of the Jaintia Hills to the north bank of the Surma river, and a small portion of the southern bank, called the 'Seven Reaches'.[2] Captain Fisher, the Superintendent of Cachar, while surveying southern Jaintia, reported in 1832 that the territory had an area of about 650 square miles with a population of 150,000 of whom the greater number were Muslims and low-caste Hindus of Bengal.[3]

Status of Bengali Language

The Bengali language enjoyed a special status in southern Khasi and Jaintia Hills because it formed the link language between the Khasi rulers and their subjects in the plains. The location of the capital of Jaintia at Jaintiapur deep in Surma Valley in the medieval period promoted Bengali as the language of the court for administrative convenience. During his march through Jaintia in April 1824 from Sylhet to Nowgong, David Scott had the occasion to visit Raja Ram Singh and the Court of Jaintiapur. He noticed that "the current language is the Bengali in which all business was carried on."[4] The report of the Agent also testifies to the hold of Bengali language on Jaintiapur. "In case of the Jynteeah family", Scott observed "the descendants of the reigning Rajas appear to gain admission in course of time into the Kayt and Bayd castes by intermarriages with individuals of those tribes, and they follow in every respect the customs of the Hindu of the plains. Persons of this origin are settled in considerable numbers about the capital and usually enjoy offices of state."[5]

Jaintiapur, as a celebrated centre of Sanskrit culture attracted a galaxy of scholars from Bengal and the Rajas of Jaintia patronised them by granting Brahmator lands. Two well known Bengali works, *Ratnavali* and *Advid Bharat,* were composed in Jaintia Darbar. The last Raja of the Jaintias, Rajendra Singh was himself a Vaisnava poet who is said to have composed devotional songs on Radha-Krishna cult that are highly popular in Sylhet.[6]

The trade and commerce, on which the hill economy was primarily dependent, also affected the promotion of Bengali language. From time immemorial the whole of the Bengal delta was fed by Khasi iron and iron products, Khasi limestone and Khasi oranges, and in their turn, Khasis fetched from the plains articles of domestic consumption, viz. rice, salt, fish, cloth, etc. The trade was confined to the Bengali speaking people of the Surma valley. The principal markets at the foot of the southern hills like Pandua, Theriaghat, Chhatak, Jaintiapur, Sonapur, etc., which lie on the navigable rivers were the feeding centres of Khasi and Jaintia Hills, and Bengali became the medium of communication between the people in the hills and the plains.

It is also worth mentioning that with the annexation of the Jaintia kingdom in 1835, the twenty-four Jaintia parganas in the southern hills that were incorporated in the Sylhet district contained a good many Khasi population. A section of them in all probability migrated to the Jaintia Hills due to the political change. Hunter, in his *Statistical Account of Sylhet* (1876-77) found 2,755 Khasis in Sylhet and this number increased to 3,083 during the Census of 1901. About the Khasis, Hunter says, "Many of these have adopted Hinduism, and obtained admission among the *Sudra* castes."[6a] The better acquaintance of these Khasis[7] of plains with Bengali language might have also been a factor in the import of this trade-cum-culture medium to their kith and kin in the southern slopes of the Khasi and Jaintia Hills. This explains the mass use of Bengali in the War areas of Khasi-Jaintia Hills, especially in Shella Sobhar and Sohra.

The use of a common language in political and commercial connections helped the growth of an intimate understanding and cordial relations between the Khasis and the Bengali Hindu. Ganga Singh by name, was installed as the Syiem of Shella. About him, Willes, the Collector of Sylhet, wrote: "Ganga Singh is a Bengali Casseah possessing territory in the hills and also holds many purganas in Sylhet formerly subject to the Mughal Government". Some Bengali Muslims from the Sylhet were also offered the Syiemship. Thus originated the Khasi state of Mawiang with Bartap Khan, Puna Khan, Jibor Khan, etc., as Syiems. Although these rulers adopted Khasi customs and Khasi way of life, they could not perhaps remain immune from the influence of the language and culture of which they had originally been the products.

Loan Words in Khasi

The Bengali was not limited to the use as a link language. It penetrated into the Khasi language itself. The loan words from Bengali constitute nearly one quarter of the Khasi vocabulary. [8] The majority of them are words for articles and customs. Thus we have (i) commercial terms like *salan* (export), *sut* (interest), *muka, rusom* (silk), *pisa* (pice), *hajar* (thousand), *lakh* (hundred thousand), *sisa* (lead), *tama* (copper), *rupa* (silver), *dukan* (shop), *saudakar* (merchant); (ii) conversational terms like *thik* (exact), *map* (forgive), *thok* (false, cheat, lie), *shalak* (clever), *shida* (simple), *kam* (work), *kamar* (blacksmith), *rukom* (custom), *riti* (custom), *khalii* (vacant), *jur* (heavy), *jaka* (place), *niam* (religion), *surok* (road); (iii) philosophical terms like *suk* (happiness), *pap* (sin), *mon* (will); (iv) names of animals like *kada* (ass), *ut* (camel), *hati* (elephant), (v) articles of domestic use like *siini* (sugar), *shun* (lime), *dut* (milk), *mithay* (molasses), *tala* (lock), *sabii* (key), *dek* (cauldron) etc. Words of Perso-Arabic origin which have entered into Khasi through Bengali include *puukir* (fakir), *mamla* (quarrel), *padsha* (emperor); *duulir* (document), *biisar* (judge), *phojdari* (case), *phasi* (hang), *phatok* (jail), *darbar* (court), *dustur* (custom), *khubor* (news), etc., etc. Instances of such loan words can be multiplied.

Use of Script

An oral tradition suggests that the Khasis had their script in ancient times which was lost in floods. The story goes that a Bengali and a Khasi swam across the river each with a book in his mouth to protect it from water. The former carried his book to the land safe, but the latter swallowed his one. So the Bengali had his literature, and the Khasi none.[9] This simple innocent tale must have originated at a time when the Khasis, before their migration to the hills, lived in the plains where flood is an occasional natural phenomenon, and it points at mutual interdependence of both the races in the plains. The tradition also suggests that at a later period, some Khasi villagers used to engage scribes called *'masoi'* who could read and write Bengali. They wrote on plantain or fan-palm leaves.[10]

The spread and popularity of Bengali were effected thus in twofold ways: first, the traders and common people of border areas carried it gradually to the Khasi courts; and second, from Darbar (court) to the neighbouring areas in the hills. The official records of the states of Sohra, Shella, Langrin, Khyrim, Mylliem, Nongstoin, Mawiang, etc. show that the Khasi Syiems used Bengali language as well as scripts for official purposes. The brass and copper seals *(mohur)* used by the states of Mylliem, Myriaw, Khyrim, and Sohra were in Bengali.[11]

Stress and Strain of Colonialism

The commercial contacts of the Khasis with the Bengalis continued even after the East India Company ascended to the Diwani of Bengal in 1765. The mercantile interest of the Company whetted when they heard about the prospect of lucrative trade in Khasi lime. "The necessities of commerce arising from their monopoly of the lime quarries from which Bengal has drawn its supply from time immemorial, soon attracted European enterprise to the country.[12] Robert Lindsay, the Resident and Collector of Sylhet showed the way by taking a lease of limestone quarries from a Khasi Syiem.[13] Legally vested with extensive powers, he was in a position to throw the sword into the scale and secure enough bargain. By this act of vandalism which went in the name of trade, Lindsay was able to convert into cash the millions of cowries in which the land revenue of Sylhet was paid. He thereby made a large fortune by means of which he had the satisfaction afterwards of earning a Peerage in London. But the Khasi-Bengali relation was damaged beyond repair by the foul play of politics of lime. In the transactions of trade, the

Company's servants depended upon their *Gomastas* and *Paikars* recruited from the plains and it is this petty business class which maintained the liaison between their new masters and the Khasi manufacturers and producers. The sturdy spirit of the mountaineers and their love of independence must have been hurt when they saw their fellow people in the plains as the camp-followers of the foreigners. The fleecing of tribal people and ruining of tribal economy roused in its sequel the wrath of the Khasis. A confrontation became inevitable, and it started with the confiscation of British merchandise on the Surma river by Chhatra Singh, Raja of Jaintia, and the capture of traders in the Company's jurisdiction. The repeated Khasi raids in the last part of the eighteenth and early nineteenth century were not mere amateur undertakings. The contemporary records are silent about the economic loss of the Khasis and their harassment by the Company's English officers and their Bengali agents. During this period the British officers were content to represent the Khasi as 'fierce marauders' and their raids have been described as 'murderous assaults' on the innocent subjects of the Company in the plains. But behind this benevolent pose of the *raj* as the protectors of plains interest, there lay the transparent design to control the overall profits of hill trade. The liquidation of Khasi trade was complete when the Khasis were excluded from the frontier markets at the foot of hills to which they had habitually resorted for the sale of their produce and purchase of grain. A string of forts was also established along the foot of the hills and permanent guards were stationed along the line of frontier dictated by the Company. The economic blockade has to be considered as the prelude to the Company's next ambitious project to annex the Khasi and Jaintia Hills. The agents of the exploiting mercantile concerns were taken by the Khasis as the representatives of the Bengali community and the segregating policy of sealing of frontier took away the possibility of a rapprochement between the hitherto two friendly neighbours. But, if the Bengali subject of the British Raj played, during this intervening period, as agents of economic exploitation to serve their master's purpose, it is interesting to note that they also supplied the Southern Khasis potential means by which the hillmen could resist the encroachment of a superior power. Hence arose the necessity of enforcing the

Regulation I of 1799 which prohibited the people of Sylhet from supplying arms and ammunition to the Khasis. Traffic in trade was, however, permitted with particular bias to promote British mercantile interests. The rise of Messrs. Inglis & Co., of Sylhet, which enjoyed the total monopoly of trade in Khasi lime and oranges, and which dictated the fate of the Khasi-Jaintia Hills in the nineteenth century, is a pointer to this fact.

First Khasi Bible

By a strange coincidence, Bengali language and a Bengali were destined to do the pioneering work in bringing Christianity to the doors of the Khasi-Jaintias. The information about the Khasis that was collected by Robert Lindsay and other residents of Sylhet through their Bengali *gomastas*, *banyans* and *paikars* reached the ears of William Carey at a time when he found his life's mission frustrated by the Company's refusal to allow any missionary work within the territory of Bengal.[14] Due to a wrong assumption that the Khasi Hills formed a link between Sylhet and the Chinese frontier, Carey sent Krishna Pal, the first Bengalee convert, to carry the Gospel to the eastern frontier of Bengal. For eight months Krishna Pal stayed at the foot of the Khasi hills at Pandua beside the Surma river preaching Christianity among the people in Bengal. The great opening he made in the work of conversion satisfied the Baptist Missionaries.[15] At Pandua, Krishna, baptised seven persons of whom two were Khasis. In his letter dated 8th May, 1813, he mentioned the names of these two Khasi converts as 'Dewan-Khasee' and 'Oona Khasi'. The ceremony of Baptism was conducted in the Bengali language and it was attended by eight Khasi Syiems and six hundred Khasi people.[16]

The District Judge of Sylhet, an English gentleman, who watched Krishna's performance with 'reverant surprise' and who built a house for him and a school room at Pandua, wrote a full account of this ceremony to Dr. Carey in his latter (dated 11 May, 1813). The extract of this letter is worth quoting as it will enable us to study the changed attitude of an English officer to the Khasi and Bengalis. After praising the services of Krishna Pal, he wrote:[17]

"I will now speak a word or two more about Pandooa, which Krishna is determined to make his headquarters...Those (Khasis) that reside on the highest parts of the mountains are very fair and handsome altogether approaching the Europeans in appearance. Such as reside towards the foot of the mountains, very much resemble the Bengali both in body and mind. They are in every repect inferior to the rest. Pandooa is the grand mart of the sale of their commodities. They trade chiefly in silks, iron, wax, honey and ivory. Their not having any written language, subjects them to great inconvenience.... They employ Bengalis to keep their accounts, and who of course can cheat them with perfect safety....The Bengalis employed by the Khasees, are called *terrovars*, or *dalals*, which answers to the English term agent. From their constant communication with the Khasees they must naturally be well acquainted with their language, manners and customs."

The report which Carey got from the District Magistrate of Sylhet and Krishna encouraged him to undertake the translation work of the Bible in Khasi language and he chose Bengali script as the medium so that the progress of the Gospel might be accelerated in the Khasi and Jaintia Hills by the 'Missionary station on its borders'.[18] With this object in view Carey was in search for a person who was well versed in Khasi language as well as in Bengali, and when he found one at last he wrote to Mr. Fuller with satisfaction:[19] "This week we obtained a person to assist in the translation of the scriptures into the Khasi language. This is an independent nation of mountaineers, lying between the eastern border of Bengal and the northern border of the Burma dominions." Thus came out, from the Serampore Mission Printing Press, *The Khasee New Testament* in 1831, a product of many years' prodigious labour. The translation which covered 898 pages was done in Bengali character. Unfortunately, the name of the translator is not yet known. Nalini Natarajan,[20] suggests that the task of translation into Khasi through the medium of Bengali alphabets was carried out with the help of a Bengali whom Carey procured from Sylhet. But this view is untenable because of the clear evidence found in Carey's biography that he believed "he (the translator) was the only one in that nation (Khasi) who could read and write".[21] In the memoir of the translation of scriptures published in 1814, the missionaries noted that "these mountaineers (the Khasis), who have a constant intercourse with the people of Sylhet, have no character of their own, nor, strictly speaking, a written language. The few among them who can read and write, use the Bengali character".[22] The Magistrate of Sylhet wrote on 20 May, 1818 to the Serampore Mission that "five or six boys, sons of rich persons and people of consequence in their tribe can be obtained through different *Rajas*" to assist in the translation of the Bible in Bengali script.[23] In view of these strong evidences, we may safely accept Dr. Bareh's opinion that "the first translator was a Khasi himself".[24]

The acquaintance with Bengali language perhaps brought the Serampore Mission a few more Khasi converts, for in the first batch of the Serampore College (1819) we find two Khasi students taking instructions with many Bengalees.[25] Dr. Carey's keen interest in the Khasi people ultimately led to the establishment of the *Khasi Hills Baptist Mission* at Cherrapunji where he sent his Bengali knowing Eurasian student Alexander Burgh Lish, after due ordination. Lish was accompanied by a young native preacher, named 'Jan', who was found "willing to be among the Bengalees".[26] Alexander Lish learnt the Khasi language and explained to the Khasis Serampore translation of the Khasi *New Testament* which was printed in "the Bengali character", and "it seemed pretty intelligible to them". [27] In 1833, Lish founded three schools in the villages around Cherra. He wrote a few school primers in Khasi and "several translations of the Gospel of Mathew and parts of the *New Testament* all of which were printed at Serampore during a visit he paid to it in 1833".[27a] A boarding school for the Khasi boys at Cherra was established by him in 1836.

But Lish probably did not succeed in procuring more Khasi converts as the initial response subsided during the Anglo-Khasi war. About the performance of Alexander Lish at Cherrapunji, *The Friend of India* [28], in its issue of 14 January, 1836, commented thus: "Hitherto no converts have been made amongst the Khasis; but this is owing as much to a determination to receive no more nominal adherence to the Gospel, as to any strong reluctance on the part of the people to renounce their own idolatry". Carey, the main inspiration behind the Khasi Mission died on 9 June, 1834, and when Alexander Lish also left Cherrapunji in 1838 due to ill health, the Baptist Missionary Society, which was not in the beginning in favour of opening a mission at Cherra, hastened to close its work.[29]

Rupture with Bengali

The vacuum caused by the closure of the Khasi Hills' Baptist Mission was filled by the Welsh Alvinist Methodist Mission (1841 AD). The first notable action of this Mission was to snap the tie of Bengali script with the Khasi language and clothe it with Roman alphabets. The rejection of Bengali script was not prompted perhaps initially by any political design, although the defeat of the Khasis in the late wars or resistance might have emboldened the Welsh Mission to take this step. Nor was the decision due to the difficulties experienced in adopting Bengali orthography for the Khasi language, because the matter had already been finally settled by Carey and his Khasi and Bengalee associates of the Serampore Mission after many years' laborious thought. The real cause for the introduction of Roman character was expediency. Thomas Jones and others who filled the cadres of the Welsh Mission were men from Wales. Unlike the Serampore Missionaries, they had no Indian background. They did not know Bengali language or script, and found it convenient to switch over to English alphabets with which they were familiar. But in doing so they ignored the traditional association of Bengali script and Bengali language with the Khasi people.

There was therefore an apparent contradiction in this policy of lamentable negligence of Bengali language and Bengali script in the educational scheme of the Welsh Mission to which the English authorities of the hills later seemed to subscribe. Since the beginning of the nineteenth century it was the East India Company which had been a principal partner in the extension of Bengali language in North East India. As a result, Bengali got an edge over the languages of Eastern India. From 1773 to 1912, Calcutta served as the capital of British India, giving the Bengalee people and Bengali language a significance and centrality unique in history. Every extension of British power at this period beyond the north-east frontier of Bengal meant an incredible push and recognition to Bengali language. The British civil officers of the Company serving anywhere in the Bengal Presidency were required to pass in Bengali. The British, again, needed, trained officials to man the *Raj* in the annexed territories and this functional need was served by the Bengalees who had the earliest opportunity of being familiar with the novel system of colonial administration.

How and why the Bengali language helped the early British civilians in establishing relations with the newly conquered territories on the frontier of Bengal can be perceived best by the career of David Scott, who did for the British in North East India what Clive did for them in Bengal, to whom the 'opening' of the Khasi and Jaintia Hills, is generally alluded. Scott had studied Bengali language and literature along with many English civilians under the guidance of Dr. William Carey and other Bengali *pandits*. Nirode K. Barooah has cited one example of Scott's knowledge of Bengali. As Commissioner of Cooch Behar, he sent Dewan Kant Bose as his agent to Bhutan in order to open up a line of communication with Tibet via Bhutan. On his return, Kishen Kant wrote an account of Bhutan in Bengali, which was translated into English by Scott himself and subsequently published in the volume, *Political Missions to Bootan* by Ashley Eden and others.[30]

(Kishen Kant also produced a work on the grammar and vocabulary of the Bhutanese language in Bengali, and on Carey's suggestions, the work was sent by Scott to Fort William College with comments that "the chief merit of the performance is the perfect accuracy with which the pronunciation of the letter and words has been marked".)

It is this acquaintance of the British civil officers with Bengali and their dependence on the Bengalee functionaries that account for the inflow of population from the districts of Sylhet, Dacca, Mymensing and Rangpur into the region. In Assam, the *Amlahs* of Bengal replaced the Ahom officials aristocracy "when the latter proved themselves incapable of discharging their duties under the alien government".[31] The same predicament befell the Khasis and

Jaintias when the new contact with colonial rule needed mass writings obviously done in Bengali language. David Scott as a part of his "grandiose imperial vision of planting European military colonies",[32] first selected Nongkhlaw as a suitable place for the sanatorium of the European officers. The use of Bengali in Nongkhlaw must have helped him in opening negotiations with U. Tirot Singh, Syiem of Nongkhlaw, with whom he concluded a treaty, which written in Bengali language, allowed the Company "a free passage for troops through his country to go and come between Assam and Sylhet".[33] From the records available to us, it appears that the Company's establishment at Nongkhlaw, after Scott had started construction, consisted of Bengali peons, *Dobhasis, Thikadars* and *Amlahs,* besides the sepoys and Assamese staff, left under the supervision of Lt. Bedingfield and Lt. Burlton. But suspicion soon arose in the minds of the freedom-loving Khasis when the real motive of the Company came to be revealed through the construction of the bungalows, an item which was not included in the original agreement. Realising that this move was a prelude to their perpetual subjection, the Khasis under Tirot Singh decided to strike. During the 'massacre' at Nongkhlaw, they spared the lives of few assamese including the *amlahs,* Mohadhar Baruah, but killed the entire Bengalee contingent whom they considered as collaborators of the White Conspiracy. The unflinching loyalty which Bedingfield's Bengalee chaprasi had shown at the time he was being dragged to the place of execution was perhaps the characteristics quality of the new class of colonial servants, making them so endeared and indispensable to their British masters. He is alleged to have told the Khasis evidently in Bengali language (which they seemed to understand): "If you kill Mr. Scott, there would come a hundred of Scotts to the burning and destruction of Nongkhlaw.[34] It was a prophecy which came true in literal sense. The English won the war by virtue of their superior arms. Tirot Singh, was deposed and the Company appointed Rujjum Singh, a lad of 13 years, as the Syiem of Nongkhlaw. The new Syiem has been described as "capable of reading and writing in Bengali then used.... as official language".[35] The Company's agreement with Rujjum Singh was recorded in Bengali and it is dated 29 March,

1834 "corresponding to the 19th of Chaitra of the Bengali year 1240".[36]

Meanwhile, Nongkhlaw was given up in favour of Saitsohpen area of Cherrapunji where a hill station and military cantonment was established, on the score of its easy accessibility from Sylhet, upon lands ceded by Raja Duwan Singh of Cherra in 1829. It is noticed that Bengali was the official language of Cherra Durbar also at this time and the Company's two agreements with Duwan Singh were recorded in Bengali and certified to be true copies by a Bengalee Vakil, Raj Kissur Mazumdar.[37] Not to speak of the Jaintia Raj, the Southern Khasi states also used Bengali script for maintenance of land records and patronised Bengali as the medium of communication with outsider. Even in 1831 at the height of Anglo-Khasi War, U. Roba of Cherra wrote a letter in Bengali to the Company's office at Sylhet pleading for the reopening of trade as its closure was causing great hardship to the Khasi people.[38] The same year saw replacement of the Persian language by Bengali and English in the Bengal Presidency.

In February 1835, Col. Lister was appointed at Cherrapunji, and the Company stuck to English and Bengali as the language of its court at Cherra. Since the administration was concerned primarily with the English and Bengalee residents of the British area and with time to time intervention in the affairs of the Khasi states, the introduction of Bengali did not pose any problem at this stage. Moreover, the states of the South Khasi Hills and Jaintia, as has been pointed out earlier, were used to Bengali language and Bengali script. The growth of the British station of Cherrapunji has been vividly described by the Baptist Missionary, Alexander Lish, in an article, "The Khasias" which he wrote at Cherrapunji in 1835, and sent for publication in the missionary paper, *Friends of India* under the pseudonym 'Monticola'.[39] In this article which was republished in the *Calcutta Christian Observer* in 1836, Lish writes :[40]

> "....operations now commenced towards providing suitable accommodations for visitors retiring for a season to Cherra for the benefit of their health. Houses were built for the reception of the expected guests, and barracks for the corps, hospital

and jail, erected. A detachment of the Bengal Artillery were sent up for sub-burnt inhabitants of Bengal repaired to the new station to taste the sweets of mountain Air."

Lish also did not fail to notice the evils of new colonial culture settling on the Khasis., According to him :[41]

"....these poor people have received no small contamination from our intercourse with them. They were sensible that they have imbibed many evils to which they were before strangers, by their communication with the Bengalis whom we have introduced among them .... Nor has the example set to them by the European inhabitants been less pernicious. From the soldiers they have learnt to drink."

The next design of the Company led to the further expansion of the British territory in the Khasi and Jaintia Hills. On the 15th March, 1835 Colonel Lister announced the annexation of the plain territory of the Jaintia Parganas possessed by the Rajas of Jaintia to the British district of Sylhet in Bengal on the pretext that Sova Singh, the Raja of Gobha, a dependency on Jaintia, had immolated, twenty years before, three British subjects at the shrine of Goddess Kali. Finding that the Company's high-handed action has not only deprived him of his only revenue earning source but also aimed at uprooting him from his cultural base, the mortified Raja Rajendra Singh renounced his claim on the hill portion of Jaintia. Gobha being annexed to the Nowgong district of Assam and Raja Rajendra Singh having surrendered the hill portion of Jaintia, the British colonisation of the Khasi and Jaintia Hills was complete.

Once the Company secured the position of paramount power in the hills, it became an imperative necessity to 'pacify' the undaunted spirit of the Khasis and Jaintias sustained so long by their small but robust republics. The British Raj, therefore, undertook such measures as would transform the indigenous institutions while providing a solid base for colonial pattern of exploitation. On the political front, this aim was achieved through successive agreements and *sanads* which reduced the Khasi Syiems and Sarkars and Jaintia

Dolois to the position of petty government officials subject to the orders and control of the highest British authority. On the economic front, the Khasis were already deprived of their low lands in the plains so indispensable for the supply of their daily necessities. The self-contained tribal economy was slowly but perceptibly transformed into an agrarian one. Forest resources, lime quarries and coal deposits belonging to the Khasi community were usurped by the Company, with the result that the people were forced to leave their trade and occupations. The development was naturally lopsided. The British colony at Cherra showed early signs of urbanisation. Timber, coal and limestone attracted European settlers. The volume of export trade alone amounted to seven lakh rupees in 1859.[42] The Inglish & Co. was the most important of the European capitalist firms which received the monopoly of trade in limestone and coal. There was so much scramble for lands in Cherra that the Government of Bengal prevented the chiefs and Sardars from making grants of lands to Europeans and other foreigners without knowledge and approval of the government.[43]

The avenues of employment both in office and trade that were opened by the British administration and European merchants of Cherra were not available to the local Khasis. At a time when the court language of the Company's government at Cherrapunji was Bengali and when the Khasi Darbars were using Bengali script to record proceedings in Khasi, the Khasis under missionary instruction lost their contact with Bengalees and were frittering their energies in learning just a muttering of the two R's (Arithmetic was beyond the scope of the missionary education syllabus, its aim being a very limited one —the propagation of Biblical knowledge). Into the big gap that was created by the missionary policy of education, entered the new comers from Sylhet, who, having the advantage of receiving free vernacular education then in vogue in Bengal, made the revenue and judicial departments their sole preserve. Since the establishment at Cherra was then small and the supply of recruits could easily be met from the neighbouring district of Sylhet, the East India Company's attitude towards education of the hill people at this earlier stage of colonisation was one of total indifference, and this explains perhaps the reason why they not only overlooked the introduction of Roman script but also entrusted the formal education of the Khasi people to the absolute care of the Welsh Mission.

The Welsh missionaries either failed to notice or totally ignored the tie of the Bengali language with the Khasis and Jaintias, its importance as the centre of political pool, its value to the Khasis as the link language for trade and commerce with Sylhet. Devoted to the pious cause of evangelism and conversion as they were, they thought, perhaps, that the purpose of the Gospel, hitherto to the Khasis would be best served by cutting off the mighty descendants of Tirot Singh and Rajendra Singh from the Indian context and pushing them into cloistered pockets where no ripple from the mainstream of Indian culture could reach on the mental plane because of barrier of script.

Khasi Reaction to Roman Script

The abandonment of the Bengali script and the introduction of the Roman was strongly resented by the Khasis. At Shella the people even made attempts to burn down the missionary school.[44] The Khasi felt no initiative to send their children to the school where Bengali had no room, while the Jaintias even considered it an attack on their tradition.[45] The lack of response to education during the period from 1841–1860 is to be ascribed to the replacement of the Bengali script by Roman. This point was emphasised by William Robinson, the Inspector of Schools. In 1856 he wrote in the *Calcutta Review*:[46]

> "The Serampore Missionaries gave the preference to the Bengali character which they found quite adequate to express all the sounds of the language and it is great pity we think that the Roman character, surrounded by a hallow of dots and dashes, has been substituted in its stead."

Robinson, who had published the grammar of Assamese language, also pleaded for the retention of Bengali script in Khasi and Jaintia Hills on ground of commercial relations of the Khasis with the plains people. "One of the objects in teaching the Khasis the arts of reading and writing", he pointed out, "is doubtless to give them a greater facility of intercourse with the people of the plains, with whom, in their commercial dealing, they are now brought into almost daily intercourse. The Bengalee character, as used at it is by the people of Sylhet on the one side, and those of Assam on the other, would have been to them a much more useful character to have adopted".[47] Commenting on the slow pace of education in Welsh Mission schools, Hudson, the Principal Assistant Commissioner, felt in 1858 that "these schools would have met with less opposition and greater success, had instruction been given in the Bengali language, and even had the Bengali instead of the Roman characters been used in writing the Cossyah language".[48]

The Government did not pay any heed to the protest of the Khasis since the policy of the Welsh Mission fitted very well with its policy of 'pacifying' the hill tribes. In the hills it gave up the policy of 'religious neutrality' which is pursued in the plains. The work of the Welsh Mission for conversion of the Khasis and Jaintias through the medium of education was appreciated by the British civil and military administration, and when the Wood's Despatch of 1854 had recommended the encouragement of education in schools on grant-in-aid basis, the Governor-General, Lord Dalhousie sanctioned a grant of Rs. 50 to the Welsh Mission which was raised to Rs. 500 p.m. in 1861.[49] Meanwhile, the government having felt contented that the subjugated people had become sufficiently the district of Khasi-Jaintia Hills was integrated in the administration of Assam. The Commissioner of Assam remained simultaneously incharge of Khasi-Jaintia Hills in his capacity as the Agent to the Governor-General. But the sweet hopes and expectations of the government were soon belied by a mass uprising in the Jaintia Hills when the Jaintias, or the Pnars as they are called, made a determined bid to overthrow the foreign yoke. Although the new taxation policy as recommended by A.J.M. Mills and W.J. Allen was primarily responsible for the Jaintia War of Liberation (1860-64), the use of Roman script and the policy of conversion so assiduously followed by the Welsh Mission were no less an important factor. After the establishment of the missionary school at Jowai "the Syntangs were told they must be Christians, and give up their time honoured *pujas* and that parents not sending their children to school and any one worshipping or divining according to old usages would soon come to grief".[50] The incident also throws light on the vicious nature of colonial administration at Cherra where 'extortion, oppression and corruption of every sort' were practised. Commenting on the sad experience of the Jaintias with the Cherra Court, J.C. Haughton the Commissioner, wrote:[51]

> "....They (Syntengs) did not know a word of the Court language, and all, as ignorant of laws entirely dependent on and at the mercy of the native officials who did not hesitate to grow rich at their expense."

Revivalism

The calculated policy of the colonial rulers to isolate the Khasis from their neighbours in the plains and to delink them from the social roots before long called upon a section of the Khasi intellectuals to endeavour to preserve the indigenous culture and the linguistic tie with the Bengalee neighbours. This awakening found its expression through a literary movement initiated by Babu Jeebon Roy who may be regarded as the apostle of the Khasi Renaissance. Born at Cherrapunji in 1838, Babu Jeebon was the first Khasi to enter the government service and to be promoted to the rank of a Senior E.A.C. His father, Ram Singh, who had business connections with Calcutta, earned the nickname 'Kerkata' because of his proficiency in Bengali as spoken in Calcutta.[52] This background had a strong influence on Jeebon who had no formal education but mastered English, Bengali and Sanskrit, besides chaste Khasi acquired a profound knowledge in Hindu classics like *Geeta, Upanishada, Ramayana, Mahabharata* and other master pieces in Sanskrit and Bengali religion literature. He came into close contact with the *Brahmo Samaj* that had appointed a permanent representative in the person of Babu Nilmoni Chakravarty in the Khasi Hills. He also examined the Khasi religion thoroughly and gained a strong insight into Khasi and Hindu religion. "The study of the religious classics of India inspired Roy with an intense pride in his Khasi and Indian heritage, which he sought to defend against the insidious propaganda of the Christian missionaries among the Khasi tribals."[53] As the Khasi had regular trade connections with Sylhet he wanted that the Khasi should learn Bengali, in addition to Khasi vernacular. He stood for secular higher education as against Welsh Mission's scheme of limited primary education (with the single exception of an M.E. School at Shillong) and the text books with Christian bias to use education as the media for the propagation of Christianity at the colonial patronage. Babu Jeebon Roy had a number of close associates among the prominent Bengalee residents of Shillong, most of whom were government servants and were inspired by the reformist and modernising spirits of the Bengal Renaissance. Their immediate demand was for a high school, and requested Rev. Thomas Jones of the Welsh Mission to upgrade the Mission M.E. School. But the Reverend replied: "We have come here for religion and not education."[54] This perhaps explains the attitude of the mission to which the Government had passed over the entire charge of education in the Khasi-Jaintia Hills and extended financial assistance from the public treasury. Jeebon Roy and his Bengalee friends then started a High School at Shillong and appealed to the Government for assistance: but the grant-in-aid was extended only after Babu Jeebon had deposited Rs. 900 towards security. Babu Sibcharan Roy, the eldest son of Jeebon Roy, was the first Khasi to pass the Entrance Examination of the Calcutta University from this school and to proceed to Calcutta for higher education in the Presidency College. The achievement of the school and its increased popularity incurred most serious concern of the government and the Mission, particularly when the enrolment in the Mission M.E. School marked gradual fall. The two schools were ultimately amalgamated into the Shillong Government High School at the initiative of the Government. In the meantime, Babu Nilmoni Chakravarty of the *Brahmo Samaj* also extended his support to the educative and reforming efforts of Babu Jeebon Roy and others. Jeebon Roy then started two Bengali schools, one in Shella and another in the *Brahmo Samaj* Hall at Mawkhar, Shillong. Like the Shillong High School, he appointed Bengalee teachers in these two schools as well and Khasi was taught side by side with Bengali.

Babu Jeebon himself wrote Khasi and Bengali primers for the schools and used Khasi tales and fables in the texts. His *Ka Kitap Chaitanya, Ka Ramayan, Budhadev Charitra, Hitupodesa, Ka Niom Ki Khasi, Shaphang Uwei U Blei,* etc., were based on Khasi religion and translations from Bengali and Sanskrit. He believed that Bengali character was more appropriate for Khasi language and some of his writings in Khasi were in that character. He started the first printing press in Khasi Hills, and taught the Khasis modern crafts, farming and gardening for social, educational and economic advancements of the Khasis as a check to the colonial and missionary exploitations.

The noble tradition set by Babu Jeebon Roy was carried by a number of Khasi intellectuals and notable of them were his two sons, Sibcharan Roy and Chandranath Roy. Babu Chandranath was the founder Secretary of Seng Khasi, a socio-cultural organisation of the Khasis that has to its credit the commendable success in preserving values of traditional Khasi religion and culture by inspiring the Khasis with a pride in their own heritage at a time the indigenous culture and institutions were on the verge of extinction due to colonial and conspiracy. Proficient in Sanskrit and Bengali like his father, Sibcharan Roy studied the Hindu classics in original and translated *Bhagavad Gita, Chanakya Niti Darpan* etc. in Khasi and wrote *Ka Niam Tip Briew Tip Blei, Ka Kot Tokit Tit Tit, Ka Jingrwai Niam Khasi,* etc., on Khasi religion and culture, besides editing the newspapers *U Nongphira* and *U Nongpynim.* Radhon Singh Barry and Hormu Roy Diengdoh figure prominently among the Khasi intellectuals in the closing years of the nineteenth century. The latter's *U Khasi Mynta* championed the cause of traditional Khasi culture, and through its columns both of them pointed out the mis-spelling of the Khasi words in Roman character by the missionaries. Hormu Roy in an article, published in the Bengali pointed out the link between Sanskrit and Khasi languages.[55] Radhon Singh and Harom Kishor Singh, who were earlier converted to Christianity, were associated with the *Brahmo* Movement of Nilmoni Chakravarty in the Khasi Hills where the preachings were done in Bengali and Khasi.[56] Harom Kishor later on started the Khasi

Unitarian Mission and was also supported by Nilmoni Chakravarty and Radhon Singh. As a matter of fact, Seng Khasi, *Brahmo Samaj* and Unitarian Church worked in close co-operation with each other, and were later on joined by Ramakrishna Mission which inspired the Khasis with the values of indigenous culture, and Khasi and Bengali formed part of its educational schemes.[57]

Nevertheless, the revivalist movement initiated by Jeebon Roy succeeded in creating the cultural consciousness among the Khasis and preserving the indigenous institutions that is being appreciated by all sections of the Khasis. His appreciation of the Bengali script for Khasi language and knowledge of the Khasis in Bengali language will remain in history as the views of one who was well versed in both the languages. But the dismissal of the Bengali script and language by the Welsh Missionaries was complete to the satisfaction of the British authorities. The colonial close-door policy in the hills succeeded in snapping the traditional tie of the Khasis with their Bengalee neighbours through the medium of script and language that had facilitated the promotion of trade and commerce to the economic prosperity of the Khasi-Jaintias. The Khasi literature, therefore, could take very little from its counterparts in Bengal and Assam, and, during the colonial period, the students were introduced to ideas more from the west than Indian or Khasi. It was due to the personal efforts of Jeebon Roy, Sibcharan Roy, Homiwell Lyngdoh, Soso Tham and few others that indigenous tales and fables and traditions could be incorporated in the literature. The so-called European tales of modern Khasi literature, who avoided the pains of gaining familiarity with Bengali script, had no anxiety to see that indigenous culture finds its expression through local literature. Twenty-four of the twenty-six Roman alphabets with tampered pronunciation of a few and two more modified with 'dots and dashes' in the words of Robinson, were found suitable for giving expression to the eastern language of the Khasis; whereas the Bengali script, with 52 alphabets and host of additional characters, were dismissed by the educators from the Wales on the plea that the simple Roman character would be easier to follow. No wonder, the tremendous progress in the field of literature witnessed in the neighbouring plains of Assam and Bengal in the nineteenth century had very little to contribute to the literary tradition of the Khasis.

NOTES AND REFERENCES

1. Hamlet Bareh, *The History and Culture of the Khasi People,* p. 117.
2. R.B. Pamberton, *Eastern Frontier of British India,* p. 223.
3. A.S.R. *Bengal Government Papers,* File No. 336 of 1835; J.B. Bhattacharjee, *Cachar Under British Rule in North East India,* p. 106.
4. R.B. Pamberton, *op. cit.* p. 226.
5. *Ibid.,* p. 228.
6. J.B. Bhattacharjee, "Sources of the History of the Khasis and, Jaintias", *cf.* S.P. Sen (ed), *Sources of the History of India,* Vol. II, pp. 214-15.
6 W.W. Hunter, *A Statistical Account of Assam,* Vol. II, p. 277.
7. Quoted in Hamlet Bareh, *op. cit.* p. 106.
8. Lily Rebel, *Khasi, A Language of Assam,* p. 38.
9. William Robinson, "The Khasi Hills", *Calcutta Review*, No. LIII, September 1856, p. 82.
10. Nalini Natarajan, *Missionary among the Khasis,* p. 115.
11. J.B. Bhattacharjee, *op. cit.,* p. 208; Hamlet Bareh, *op. cit.,* p. 294.
12. W.W. Hunter, *A Statistical Account of Assam,* Vol. II, p. 234.
13. *Ibid.,* p. 351.
14. S.P. Carey, *The Life of William Carey,* p. 356.
15. Periodical Accounts, Serampore Mission.
16. "An Account of Krishna Pal, as given by himself", *The Annual Report of the Baptist Mission Society,* Serampore, 1823, p. 35.
17. Periodical Accounts, Serampore Mission, No. XXVII, pp. 227-29.
18. *Ibid.,* No. XXIX, p. 655.
19. *Ibid.,* No. XXVII, p. 399, Carey to Fuller, 14 December, 1813.
20. Nalini Natarajan, *op. cit.,* pp. 60-61.
21. S.P. Carey, *op. cit.,* p. 408.
22. Periodical Accounts, Serampore Mission, No. XXIX, p. 623.
23. Quoted in Hamlet Bareh, *op. cit.,* p. 397.
24. *Ibid.*
25. S.P. Carey, *op. cit.,* p. 332.
26. E.S. Wenger, Missionary Biographies, Mss,. in Serampore Mission Library, pp. 105-6.
27. *Ibid.,* p. 106.
27 E.S. Wenger, *op. cit.,* p. 106.
28. *The Friend of India,* Vol. II, No. 55, 14 January, 1836.

29. *The Annual Report of the Committee of the Baptist Mission Society,* Serampore, 1839, p. 22.
30. Nirode K. Barooah, *David Scott in North East India,* p. 16fn.
31. H.K. Barpujari (ed), *Political History of Assam,* Vol. I, p. 62.
32. Nirode K. Barooah, *op. cit.,* p. 211.
33. M.L. Bose, *History and Constitutional Documents of North East India,* No. 9 "Agreement of Tirot Singh of Nongkhlaw, 1826", p. 90,: Hamlet Bareh, *The Language and Literature of Meghalaya,* p. 56.
34. R.M. Lahiri, *Annexation of Assam,* p. 73.
35. M.L. Bose, *op. cit.,* No. 10 "Agreement of Rujjum Singh of Nongkhlaw", p. 92.
36. *Ibid.*
37. *Ibid.,* No. 2 "Agreement with Dewan Singh, 1829", p. 83.
38. Hamlet Bareh, *op. cit.,* p. 56.
39. *The Friend of India,* April 2, 1835.
40. Rev. A.B. Lish, "A Brief Account of the Khasis", Calcutta, *Christian Observer,* March 1838.
41. *Ibid.*
42. H.K. Barpujari, *Problem of Hill Tribes: North East Frontier,* Vol. II, p. 74.
43. M. L. Bose, *op. cit.*
44. Nalini Natarajan, *op. cit.*
45. P.N. Dutta, "Emergence and Role of the Middle Class in the Khasi-Jaintia Hills", paper presented in a Seminar on *Middle Class in North East India,* NEICSSR, Shillong, 1978.
46. William Robinson, *op. cit.,* p. 81.
47. *Ibid.*
48. Quoted in Kynpham Singh, "Khasi and Jaintia Hills upto 1874", *Shillong Century Celebration Souvenir,* p. 6.
49. Hamlet Bareh, *History and Culture of the Khasi People,* p. 442.
50. H.K. Barpujari, *op. cit.* p. 80.
51. *Ibid.,* p. 79 fn.
52. U. Khasi Mynta, Khasi Monthly, Jyllew, 1903, Ka Jingialang Kynmaw (Booklet issued on the occasion of the 39th Death Anniversary of U. Jeebon Roy), Shillong, 1933, p. 8.
53. S.P. Sen (ed), *Dictionary of National Biography,* Vol. III, p. 556.
54. *Golden Jubilee Souvenir,* Ramakrishna Mission, Cherrapunjee, 1974, pp. 57-58.
55. Quoted in Kynpham Singh (ed), *Ki Kat Ba La Thoh Da Ki Khasi,* pp. 17-19.
56. Nilmoni Chakravarty, *Atmajibansmriti,* pp. 124-76.
57. J.B. Bhattacharjee, "The Messenger of Khasi Heritage". *Khasi Heritage,* Shillong, 1979, pp. 1-28.

3

EVOLUTION OF ASSAMESE AS A MEDIUM OF INSTRUCTION

M. Kar

Assam had contact with Bengal in ancient times. The Ahom kings also encouraged people to settle here as artisans, weavers, clerks, scholars and divines etc. Inflows of people from Bengal continued in driplets over a span of nearly five centuries of attempted Muslim conquests. They settled mostly in the Brahmaputra Valley. Major portions of Cachar and the whole of Sylhet and Goalpara, all Bengali speaking areas, came under Assam administration in 1874.

British Policy-Pragmatism: Following the Treaty of Yandabow, 1826, the East India Company at first tried to establish its hegemony in Assam through a puppet king. But that experiment failed and then the Company annexed Assam and placed the territory under Bengal Administration. The establishment of the Company's authority, the consequent necessity of manning the different departments of government and the reconstitution of Assam bringing in large Bengali speaking areas, may be taken to be the beginning of the language problem. But it was then a problem of finding educated persons for an administrative machinery of the expanding British empire in India. A good number of Bengalees, already conversant in the art of Government, came to the Province on various assignments, in the interest of British administration to replace the 'indolent' and incapable nobility of the earlier regime.[1]

Persian was the court language of the Bengal Presidency of which Assam was then an administrative unit. Few of the new recruits in Assam knew English or Persian. "In April, 1831, the Government of Bengal made Bengali in place of Persian the court language of Assam on the ground that it was very difficult and too costly to have replacement when a Persian scribe was on leave or left the service".[2] Bengali was actually introduced in 1837. The services of the Bengalees immediately became indispensable in the Anglo-vernacular and vernacular school, since local teachers were not available in adequate numbers, in any case to impart lessons in Bengali which had since become the medium of instruction.[3] It may be mentioned here that Act XXIX of 1837 had provided for the use of the vernacular languages of a district in the Court, but the government allowed the replacement of Assamese there also. However, the missionary and indigenous schools continued to teach Assamese. The first Assamese journal '*Arunoday*' was started by the American Baptist Mission from Sibsagar in 1846.[4] The general notion engendered later on that the Bengalees were responsible for this change does not bear historical scrutiny. The need of educating the children of these subordinate Bengalee officials in their mother tongue was obvious and they might have demanded education accordingly, though there is no evidence of any organised demand. We must also note that in those days of British imperial expansion the Bengalees, as other Indians, had little say in policy determination and could only petition the authorities for any right or facility. Further, all power centres in the administrative machinery were filled by Englishmen. The Assamese had no voice as the English had come apparently as saviours and then turned devourers. To the Company, territory and good trade, consolidated through an efficient administration were of the greatest importance.

Assamese Voice Heard — Government Sympathy

With the progress of education following British occupation, the demand for restoration of Assamese as a language of education and courts was natural and justified and was for the first time voiced by Ananda Ram Dhekial Phukan.[5] A.K. Moffat Mills an officer deputed by Bengal Government to report on Assam, also clearly expressed his view in support of the language. Mills thought that the administration had made a great mistake in directing that all business should be transacted in Bengali and that the Assam had to acquire it, but it was too late to retrace the steps.[6] The first ever formal recommendation for introduction of Assamese in the courts, made by Col. Hughton, Commissioner, Assam Valley, was rejected by the Bengal Government.[7] But in the meanwhile, all Assam civil officers were compelled to pass a test in Assamese just as Bengalee Officers had to pass in Bengali thus recognising the vernacular status of Assamese, but the government showed no inclination to go further.[8] By the time of reconstitution of the Province into a Chief Commissionership in 1874, memorandums from different parts of the Brahmaputra Valley were being presented to the Government of Bengal for introduction of Assamese in the schools and courts.[9] Lt. Governor Sir George Campbell held that "the vernacular of a people ought not to be elbowed out of a country in favour of another language which happened to be the vernacular of a neighbouring more numerous and more educated people".[10]

He also observed that tendency of the Government of India and of the legislation of late years was to permit the vernacular of each Province to be its courts. He called for reports as regards language spoken in different districts of Assam and also enquired why Bengali should not be replaced by Assamese. Majority of the Deputy Commissioners, and Assistant Commissioners, except the Deputy Commissioner Goalpara, were in favour of Assamese but Col. Hopkinson, Commissioner, Assam Valley districts for 13 years prior to his retirement in 1874, and another very experienced English officer, A.E. Campbell, were in favour of retention of Bengali.[11]

Government Policy Defined

The Lt. Governor asserted that the vernacular of the province was Assamese and in a Resolution dated 19 April, 1873, he prescribed the use of Assamese in the courts. It was also decided that "In all Primary schools, Assamese will be taught to the exclusion of Bengali; also in all Middle Schools and in the Lower and Middle classes of Higher Schools. When a class of 12 or more boys wish for it, Bengali may be separately taught to them as a language. In the upper classes of Higher Schools, every subject in which there is an Assamese Book is to be taught in Assamese; subjects in which Assamese school books do not exist can be taught either in Bengali or in English."

Text Books Hurdle

He also admitted that the real difficulty in recognising Assamese was the paucity of Assamese books.[12] By this order, clearly, Bengali as medium of instruction in the lower classes of all types of schools was discarded and teaching of Bengali was allowed only as an exception rather than the rule and in higher classes, Bengali could be replaced only if books in Assamese were available. The absence of Assamese text books, however, presented an insurmountable obstacle to the operation of this order. The next year, Dr. C.A. Martin, Inspector of Schools, lamented "...The Assamese language has no literature of its own deserving the name so that at present the effect of this order is to bring education in the valley districts of the Province more or less to a standstill" and suggested that "...means should be devised to guard against the existing schools falling into a rapid decline".[13] He also pointed out that boys who went to the High Schools had to take Bengali because Sanskrit, the alternative subject, could be taught only to a specific number of students and that number was hardly ever there. As regards Goaplara, he advocated a dichotomy of policy as he asserted that the people had expressed their choice in favour of Bengali. As regards Middle Schools, higher classes of High Schools and Normal Schools, he suggested the retention of Bengali, "for in these classes the most difficult subjects will be taught and the more difficult the subjects, the more nearly must language approach to good classical Bengali".[14] This could not have been a satisfactory arrangement to the Assamese.

Luttman Johnson, Secretary to Chief Commissioner, wrote in reply that the latter adhered to Lt. Governor's decision making it obligatory to teach Assamese as a vernacular and not Bengali. The rigidity was, however, relaxed by allowing the use of the language most easily and best understood by the student and deciding that

"...if the boys understand Bengali, the Chief Commissioner has no objection to Bengali books being used. Even when they understand Bengali imperfectly, Bengali books in absence of others may be used". Another relaxation was made by allowing the teaching of Bengali as a separate language at the wishes of the Director of Public Instruction. Goalpara was excluded from the operation of this order. The Inspector of Schools was also permitted to introduce into the Primary Schools a set of primers according to his preference. In the higher classes of High Schools, specifically Bengali was retained as the medium of instruction in which other subjects, besides literature, would be taught.

Further Progress

For the next seven years no further progress was made in the matter. An Assamese primer which was earlier approved by the D.P.I. was rejected by the Chief Commissioner whose action was endorsed by the Lt. Governor on the ground that the Committee passing the book had been influenced by the Bengali element and its supporters. Sir Stuart Bayley, Chief Commissioner, in his Resolution on the Education Report 1879-80, opened the question of modification of the system with the intention of "decreasing the difficulty of the Bengali Course" and expressed desire for a reconciliation between the two interests. Obviously a conflict was visualised. But at the same time he observed that it should be the "endeavour to convince the people of the advantage of assimilating their cultivated speech as far as possible to the far more important, more highly developed language of the lower province".[15] The next Chief Commissioner, Sir Charles Elliot referred to Sir Bayley's observations and asked for a mature project from the D.P.I. The same year, the Anglo-vernacular Text Book Committee, Nowgong, which was appointed by the Government of India in 1878, recommended the retention of both the existing Bengali course and its contents for the Middle English Examinations till Assamese books were available.[16] J. Willson, D.P.I., also praised the then existing system as providing a sound instruction in Bengali.[17]

The Government was more interested in educating people in Bengali and cared less for Assamese. The matter of replacing Bengali by Assamese in the schools of the Brahmaputra Valley was taken up by the D.P.I. in 1881.[18] In conformity with the Government of India's Resolution No. 101 dated 23 April, 1877, that primary education should always be in mother tongue, it was decided in 1883 that Assamese could be introduced in the schools subject to the availability of the text books which were, however, notified in D.P.I's circular No. 17 of 1885-86 and since then any aided school had the free option of taking up the full Assamese course.[19]

Within the next ten years, nine out of thirteen aided middle schools took up Assamese, three Bengali and one other school remained in indecision. In eleven Government middle schools, Bengali was the medium of instruction. In 1896, the D.P.I. claimed that instruction through the medium of Bengali was more efficient than through the medium of Assamese. Only two out of six government middle schools in the mofusils were, on petition, allowed to introduce Assamese in 1897 and the remaining four preferred to retain Bengali.[20] As regards District Headquarters schools, under orders of Chief Commissioner, Sir William E. Ward, dated 10 November, 1896, Assamese was to be introduced replacing Bengali with effect from February 1897. But the medium was to be Assamese if the parents and the guardians of the pupils of the schools so desired.[21] Thus the principle of local option was surely adopted as a new one.

Cotton's View

Sir Henry J.S. Cotton's Chief Commissionership from 1896 to 1902 witnessed a very lengthy and thorough discussion of the whole question of Assamese language, and its introduction in schools and inclusion in the university syllabus as a second language. Cotton had strong views on both these aspects of the question. As regards restoration of Assamese, he observed, "Every educated Assamese is bound to know Bengali just as every educated Welshman is bound to know English" and the cry for the restoration of Assamese as the language of culture in this Province is as hopeless as the agitation "...for the official recognition of the Welsh language in Wales". "The tendency is all in one direction and the classical literature in Assam of which apparently little remains, will in due course, be placed in the category of the writings of Cadwallon or Fingul or Ossain. All efforts to boost up Assamese as a separate language are, I am convinced, doomed to failure. He, however, conceded that as Assamese was still then the vernacular of the masses of the Province, it was the duty of the administration at least to offer the necessary encouragement in primary or even in the middle school to that language. But in the case of higher education, he maintained that all such education must be imparted through the channel of Bengali and English. "Everyday, Bengali tends to replace Assamese as the language of educated society and though it may be natural to patriotic Assamese to attempt to resist the flowing tide, the endeavour is a hopeless one", he observed. His Secretary, P.G. Melitus, however, holds a contrary view.

Cotton placed it on record as his own view that the closer Assam identified itself with Bengali, the Province from which it was administratively but an offshoot, the more rapid would be its progress and the greater the prosperity of its people. Malitus remarked that such a view would strike the people as novel and that they did not like to be swamped by Bengalees as the people of Bihar and Orissa had been under Bengal administration. But, Cotton asserted, "When this truth is fully recognised in Assam, our schools may emulate the success of a generation ago when they were able to train up scholars like the Late Anandaram Barooah". The move for recognition of Assamese as a second language in the University syllabus was also strongly opposed by him as well as by J. Willson. D.P.I. on the ground of absence of text books in the Assamese language. Cotton also thought that such a step would tend to weaken the links of union with Bengal which were to the advantage of the Assamese people themselves.[22] But in fact, those links catered to the needs of administration rather than the needs of the people in general.

Public Reaction and Government Decision

The order of William Ward was implemented in February 1897.

This was followed by the biggest ever protest memorial which was signed by three thousand three hundred and sixty-six persons. A counter memorial for extension of the scope of the order into high schools, inclusion of Assamese in the University syllabus and compulsory reading of Assamese books by Assamese boys was also presented. These steps, the counter memorialists claimed, would prevent the unhealthy interference of the Bengalees if the selection of language was left to the discretion of the Head Masters of the ignorant guardians.[23] The order of 1896 was clearly misconstrued as the parents and guardians of the pupils but not the Headmasters were given any discretion in the matter. Cotton refused to enlarge the scope of Ward's order vide his decision dated 6 December, 1897. The Bengalee petitioners had recognised the claim of Assamese and prayed for the instruction of the Bengalee boys in their own mother tongue. But the government refused to undertake the teaching of both the vernaculars and asked them to make their own arrangement. Captain Gurdon's instruction of Assamese at his own initiative in Kamrup was not disapproved.[24] The D.P.I., Dr. Booth construed by oversight the orders of the Chief Commissioner to have empowered him to introduce Assamese by his own desire only and in 1901, ordered the Headmasters of Dibrugarh, Sibsagar, Jorhat, Nowgong and Tezpur High Schools to introduce the language. Certainly this served the cause of Assamese language well. Later on he pleaded guilty of indiscretion which appeared to have been condoned by the Chief Commissioner on 8 June, 1901.[25] The same year, the Bengalee residents of Tezpur prayed for the teaching of their children in Bengali in the lower classes. Their prayer was turned down and in protest they withdrew their children and started a school of their own. But the matter proceeded no further.

J.B. Fuller and his Policy

The next Chief Commissioner, Sir J.B. Fuller, disfavoured the continued instruction in Bengali. He adopted the view that needs of the Assamese in Assam had to be preferred to those of the Bengalees.[26] This was a clear deviation from the Government of

India's policy which admitted of no preferential treatment but stressed the principle of education through the medium of mother tongue; the principle was, of course, adopted long after the change in Assam's language had been made for the first time.

Voluminous opinions were received from District and Sub-Divisional Officers as also from the Commissioner, Assam Valley and private individuals, both Assamese and Bengalees, for and against the language as the medium of instruction. Some of the representative opinions are summarised here.

The Commissioner of Assam Valley generally agreed with Fuller but favoured some relaxation for Bengalees in consideration of large number of 'intelligent' Bengalee population in some places. He also observed: "...in giving instruction in Assamese instead of Bengali, we are sacrificing something of efficiency. I have no doubt that better education can be given through the medium of Bengali." He was in doubt about text books being written on demand and commented that "...at any rate, the Assamese text books will probably be inferior to those which will be available in Bengali". British officers preference in the matter has always been ignored in all discussions about Assam's language problem and the Bengali aspect has been over-emphasised.

Fuller deviated again both from the existing arrangement and the University Regulation as he ordered on 14 August, 1903, that "... in future in the Assam Valley, excluding Goalpara District, Bengali will not be taught as a second language for the University Entrance Examination nor (subject to possible exception at Gauhati) will it be used as a medium of instruction in classes below the fourth. These orders should apply to aided schools as well as to Government High Schools and *mutatis mutandis*, to Middle Schools..." so that the Bengalee teachers might not suffer, the Chief Commissioner decided to transfer them gradually either to Goalpara or to the Surma Valley. In consideration of the inconvenience that might be felt by the Bengalees, he was prepared to help them financially if they wanted to have schools for their boys upto the fourth class. Thus, the principle of local option was narrowed down practically to a nullity. As regards text books, he was certain that such books would be written if there was a demand for them. Paucity of suitable text books is, however, still now admittedly a problem. Apparently, Fuller's orders had solved the problem except in Goalpara. But Goalpara defied such simplification as Fuller's formula and in course of time the problem of language in the district with a dominant Bengalee population got intricately mixed with Assam politics.

The Problem in Goalpara— D.C.'s *death sentence on Assamese language:* The Deputy Commissioner, Goalpara was strongly opposed to the Assamese language as "...practically only Bengali is here spoken." He thought that "...it is very little use fostering a language like Assamese spoken as it is, by only 36,00,000 and absolutely useless outside the five districts of upper and middle Assam. It would be far better that Assamese as a language should cease to exist and that Bengali should take its place...", an extreme view indeed, never expressed by any advocate of Bengali language. He also observed that for a really thorough education, a thorough knowledge of Bengali was necessary and Assamese had practically no literature ancient or modern and no newspapers, scientific books and novels etc. Early familiarisation of the Assamese boys with the Bengali language and instruction in Bengali can "...best give them what is wanting in their own..."[27] Side by side with the extreme views of the Chief Commissioner and the Deputy Commissioner, Goalpara, we find a spirit of compromise which was best illustrated in a resolution passed in a Dibrugarh meeting held in 1903 under the Chairmanship of an Assamese, Jaduram Baruah. Bengalees present here had no objection to Assamese being introduced in the schools of Assam if Bengali was not altogether excluded. Also the Assamese di[d not] object to Bengali remaining as a second language if arrangem[ents] could be made to teach them separately.[28] Thus the problem now boiled down to a mutual tolerance at least in a vocal section of the Brahmaputra Valley, but, unfortunately, this was a feeble voice. In 1905, the Calcutta University recognized Assamese as a second language for the Entrance Examination.[29]

The controversy in Goalpara went on. It may be interesting to note that on 19 February, 1912 a resolution for introduction of

Assamese in certain schools of the Goalpara sub-division on an experimental basis, was moved by a Bengali gentleman and passed by a majority of votes.

It was opposed on the ground that the change of a language was a matter of policy to be determined by the educational authorities. It may be recollected here that according to the existing orders of 1898, local option was prerequisite to any such change. Protest memorials were sent by some Bengalees. The cause of Assamese was taken up by a gentleman of Jorhat who sent a petition along with a booklet in Assamese, pleading for its introduction there. It was thus no longer a district issue. Accepting his Secretary's advice the Chief Commissioner sent him a reply only expressing interest in the progress of the language but passed no orders to modify the existing arrangement. A lengthy debate, however, ensued among the high officials. Both sides quoted ethnic, linguistic and political history of Assam in favour of their claims. The most hair-splitting arguments came from Lt. Col. P.R.T. Gurdon, Commissioner, Assam Valley. He extremely complicated the problem by injecting into it types of dialects spoken, religious conversion and utilisation of the ignorant Muslims by the Bengali Hindus etc., and pleaded the cause of Assamese.

J.R. Cunningham, D.P.I. tried to meet the arguments of Gurdon by quoting from the same sources as those of the latter and concluded that Goalpara belonged to Bengal and Bengali should be its vernacular. Even admitting a greater affinity of Assamese language with the language evolved by local usages, he would not agree to divide the district linguistically "... with Bengali as the Court and School language in the west and Assamese in the East". Observing that the Sub-divisional boundaries shown on the map did not conform to the actual distribution of the respective language groups, he suggested that a correction would involve interchange of certain places between the two Sub-divisions of Goalpara and Dhubri. This was perhaps the first clear expression in India of the principle of linguistic redistribution of administrative units. Cunningham further commented that all the ethnological, historical and linguistic arguments, and the decision of some ignorant people could not decide the issue but only indicated their respective social and political sympathies. Thus, he was opposed to transformation of the problem into a field of public agitation led by person well acquainted with Bengali, English and Assamese.

This debate was concluded by Chief Commissioner, Sir Archdale Earle in his order dated 16 January, 1914, deciding that the medium of instruction " ...in schools of all classes throughout the Goalpara District should be either Assamese or Bengali at the option of the majority of the villagers interested." Thus, specially extending the principle of local option to Goalpara.[30] In an explanatory note, the Chief Commissioner rejected Col. Gurdon's suggestion to allow the Deputy Commissioner or an European Officer or a particular Assamese gentleman to go round the villages to ascertain the wishes of the parents. His suggestion to allow the Deputy Commissioner to determine any dispute regarding the language was also not accepted. The Chief Commissioner directed that no change would be allowed unless it was applied for and granted. He was anxious that such approved change should be effected as quickly as possible and that "... greatest possible care should be taken not to stir up faction or feeling in the district... ". Now, the majority of the villagers—and not necessarily only parents and guardians of the pupils—could make the language a medium of instruction.

New Complication—How Government tackled: But this uniformity of policy could not be worked as by this time the Muslims had become vocal about their separate interests and demanded the introduction of an Islamic course of studies. The Muhammadan Education Conference of 1914 had recommended the introduction of an Islamic course but did not favour instruction in Urdu in ordinary lower Primary schools. In the Government policy enunciated in Education Department Notification No. 41 of 27 September, 1915, it was decided that as an experiment, facilities would be provided for the teaching of Koran in ordinary vernacular schools. For further popularising the schools amongst the Muslims, the teaching of Urdu as an optional subject for the Muslim boys was permitted.[31]

Another factor came into play within a few years. For some time the leaders of Goalpara were trying for reunion of the district with Bengal from which it was severed in 1874. Raja Prabhat Chandra Barua of Gauripur, one of the supporters of the demand, had taken pride in calling himself an Assamese at the time of formation of the Assam Association at the beginning of the century. But his view, as of many others changed soon. The famous Ninth Despatch shows that during the controversy over the extension of the scope of Montague-Chelmsford Reforms to Assam, the same Prabhat Chandra Barua submitted on behalf of the zamindars of Goalpara a very lengthy memorial to the Chief Commissioner of Assam requesting him for transfer of the District to Bengal. One of his arguments was that "the people of Goalpara, with a small exception, speaks the Bengali language and their manners and customs are the same as those of the people of Northern Bengal." Further, according to him 4,40,408 out of a total population of 6,00,643 spoke Bengali : the "...predominant written language is Bengali", there was an increase of one and a half lakh in the Bengalee population since 1911 Census and "that as regards history, tradition, social and religious customs and folk music, the people of the district of Goalpara have very little in common with the people of the other districts of Assam." The Hindus were interested in transfer, the Muslims emphasized Islamic education.

The Conference of Education Officers, held in 1921 recommended the establishment of thrity-one schools for the children of the immigrant Muslims, twelve immediately and the rest later. They also recommended the addition of Urdu to the Elementary course of Islamic instruction. A Primary School with only Muslim boys was to be called a *Muktab*. Each school would have two teachers, one for vernacular and the other Maulvi. Further, the schools would be under the government and not under the Local Boards. The D.P.I. objected to the introduction of Urdu as running counter to the recommendation of 1914. He was also against appointment of a separate teacher for religious instruction at State expenses and to the provincialisation of those schools as Primary schools were already under the Local Boards. He advocated the policy of equal treatment to all Muslims, immigrant or others, in both the valleys.[32] Clearly the evolution of a sound education policy, both secular and religious, i.e. a dichotomy of the existing arrangement brooked no delay.

Government Policy: The Government policy as expressed by B.C. Allen, Commissioner, Assam Valley, was to assimilate these Muslims to the native population. So far as Goalpara and the Muslims—the bulk of whom were Bengalee immigrants—were concerned, it became impossible for government to pursue a straightforward policy. Allen said "....the instruction should be in Assamese which is the country of their adoption." But he cautiously suggested ...the use of Assamese where it was not strongly objected to and did not influence the immigrants against sending their children to schools, the Government decided generally to endorse the Commissioner's views. But where a school was situated in the midst of the immigrant *bustees*, the language of instruction would be vernacular of the immigrants. In other places of Assamese predominance the language would be Assamese, each case being decided on merit. This only conformed to the policy of local option.[33] But the problem was now coloured by religious and racial sentiments.

Hierarchy and the Problem: Under the Montague-Chelmsford reforms, education became a transferred subject and the matter came to popular representatives in the Legislative Council for decision. The general policy already enunciated was not tampered with. But the Education Minister, Rai Bahadur Promode Chandra Dutta, a Bengalee from Surma Valley, decided on 27 October 1923 that "...where local opinion is substantially strong, provision should be made for reaching in both the languages." He also allowed the local Boards discretion to have Assamese or Bengali or both the languages in their schools. Sayed Muhammad Saadulla, the next Education Minister, an Assam Valley Muslim, also accepted this view but according to him, application for change of language had to come from the villagers and not merely from the parents and guardians of the pupils. He also denied school committees the power to determine the language. The Goalpara Local Board's Resolution noted earlier was not, however, undone.

Saadulla's view created complications. Difference of opinion regarding the meaning of majority and the procedure of determining the majority wishes took another five years to be settled. In 1925,

Saadulla admitted in reply to a question in the Legislative Council that "... Goalpara is a bilingual district..." and asserted that the government policy of 1914 was still being followed. On receipt of allegations of partiality and propaganda in favour of Assamese language by Assamese officers, the Government in 1927 asked all officers to maintain a neutral attitude to the language controversy. Saadulla then brought the matter to the notice of the Governor, Sir L. Hammond, as he thought the whole question involved a vital and important policy of Government.[34]

The Governor accepted Saadulla's views as sound and deplored the continuous agitation on language in the Goalpara district when the need of the hour was the removal of illiteracy. As regards both the languages being taught in the same school, he ordered on 30 January, 1929, that a minority demanding extra teacher would have to bear the expense. He would not also allow the Chairman of the Local Board to change a language without previously taking expert opinion of the Education Department who would take "... every step possible to ascertain the wishes of the majority of the villagers or persons...". The Local Board would have to ensure such consultation.[35] This decision put the Bengalees to a disadvantage.

Conflicting Attitude: As this stage, Chandradhar Barooah of Jorhat Sarbajanik Sabha, in a memorial, lamented that the Assamese language was being driven out of Local Board Schools in Goalpara district and appealed to the Governor for action. In a counter memorial, Saifur Rahman, ex-member of the Assam Legislative Council, Member, Goalpara Local Board and President, Anjuman-i-Islamia, Goalpara, challenged Barooah's contention and said that "... the language of the Division is no doubt Assamese, but Bengali is the prevailing language of the district which required as much protection as any other language." He also complained of unauthorised changes in language and the complaint seemed partially corroborated by the necessity of Government's cautioning their officers and the Governor's laying down of rigid restriction on change of language and that the Sabha was trying to exterminate Bengali root and branch from Goalpara. He also claimed that an enquiry would prove the existence of a systematic campaign for imposition of Assamese on the Bengalees. This has been a persistently typical example of the two attitudes involved in the language controversy in Assam.[36]

Since 1937 : In 1937, the Brahmaputra Valley had a total of three thousand three hundred and seven Primary schools against three thousand five hundred and fifty-nine in Surma Valley. Of these, Goalpara had seven hundred and twenty-three, the largest number, second only to Kamrup. Altogether two hundred and seventy-eight schools of all classes in the Brahmaputra Valley continued to impart education in Bengali, two hundred and sixty-seven being in Goalpara alone.[37] During the next decade, as represented by the Bengalees to the State Reorganization Commission and claimed in the Assembly on 17 November, 1955, the number of Bengali Primary schools in Goalpara had dwindled to three only by that year.

In this context a statement made by Phani Bora, a veteran Assamese Communist leader at a press conference at Gauhati on 27 May 1954 is worth quoting. He said : "The Assam Government through their official and non-official agents forcibly sealed off all Bengali schools in Goalpara district denying safeguards of the Bengalees' cultural and linguistic rights. Such imperialist and reactionary actions of the Assam Congress Government were responsible for encouraging disintegrating elements in Assam..."

Same Old Problem: In 1937, the Calcutta University introduced vernacular as a medium of instruction in the Matriculation Examination. There was a just demand for Assamese as a medium of instruction also in Assamese High Schools for the purpose. The Education Minister of the first popular ministry under the Government of India Act, 1935, led by Saadulla, stated in the Assembly on 4 August, 1937 that funds were provided for the production of suitable Assamese text books due to paucity of which the introduction of Assamese as a medium had to be postponed—the same old argument after 32 years. But he asserted that Bengali vernacular as medium had been introduced in 1937 itself.[38] Assamese was recognised by the Calcutta University as a subject in M.A. Examination in 1938. As admitted by Sir Saadulla, the Premier in 1940, Assamese had become the medium of instruction in the

Brahmaputra Valley, except Goalpara and the Bengali schools both in the Middle and Secondary standards. At the same time, however, Rohini Kumar Choudhury, Education Minister stated that Bengali schools were being started in Nowgong till then.[39] The old problem of suitable text books in Assamese remained unsolved and translations from Bengali books had to be used. In 1941, a Brahmaputra Valley Assamese Member asked in the Provincial Legislature: "Are the Government aware of the undesirability of introducing translation of Bengali books where original Assamese books are available?" Rohini Kumar Choudhury replied: "Yes, if the original Assamese books are at least as good as the translations of Bengali books". During the War years the question of language was more or less dormant.

After Partition; "One of the reasons why the Assamese supported the separation of Sylhet was that they would be able to establish the predominance of their language. Immediately after partition, Assamese leaders became more vocal about the position of their language and culture, and demanded the introduction of Assamese in the province as a whole and its adoption as the state language."

On 26 September, 1947, the Bardoloi Government directed that "... Assamese is accepted as compulsory second language in all schools where it cannot be Assamese completely." To the Bengalees' complaint of Government's partiality in the matter and imposition of Assamese on them, Gopinath Bardoloi, the Chief Minister replied on 23 March, 1948 in the Assmebly: "If you must analyse the population of Assam, you will find there is hardly any community in Assam which may be called the majority community. I do not know whether this fact is known... In Assam there is no community which may be called a majority community in which the population of one community is predominantly more than the population of another community..." Again..."as I said, there are hardly any minorities in the province and that is, I suppose, to the best interest of the Province. Nobody can rule over anybody on account of the number of any community and that has probably been one of the reasons why we have lived in such peace and unity."[40]

But participating in the debate on a cut motion to raise a discussion on the question of alleged imposition of Assamese and protection of Bengali language in Goalpara. Shri Nilmoni Phukan made a categorical assertion on 29 March, 1948 on the basis of the Premier's statement that Assam would not be a bilingual state. He said: "This question of protecting the Bengali speaking minority of Goalpara district cannot arise". Again he emphasized that it was clear from one end of the country to the other that "...geographical territory of Assam can no longer be disturbed on any other ground of linguistic basis of any minority community...Regarding our language, Assamese must be the state language of the Province (hear, hear)... There can be no gainsaying on it even if the government stand or fall on it (hear, hear). So the question of language is solved once for all. The question of language for the minority communities in Assam is also solved ...At least Assamese people as a whole will not and cannot tolerate any other language or culture imposed on theirs. All the languages of different communities and their culture will be absorbed in Assamese culture... We, the Assamese people will resist to a man and will never allow any other language to establish permanently as the state language in Assam." Claiming to speak with authority in the matter regarding the mind of the people, he asserted "...we will have Assamese alone as our State Language and the state cannot nourish any other language in this province.[41]

Bardoloi's assurance and assertions were not honoured by his successors and the good work of the past was undone. The Assamese language was restored to the position it deserved. The State Reorganisation Commission prescribed a population percentage of seventy or more for any state to be unilingual and distinctly admitted the multilingual composition of Assam. Thus, all the happenings in connection with the language during the last twenty-two years, too well known to be recounted here, were totally unwarranted from any reasonable point of view. It may be of interest to note that Shri Sarat Chandra Sinha, later Chief Minister of Assam has expressed the same view as Shri Phukan in 1948. But he had to witness the worst ever manifestation of the language malaise in 1972. Suffice it to say that the language question has become favourite expediency of the politicians and has to be sttled *de novo*.

NOTES AND REFERENCES

1. Barpujari. H.K., *Assam in the Days of the Company,* p. 46.
2. *Ibid.*, 266.
3. *Ibid.*
4. Assam Secretariat File (A.S.F.) No. 171G of 1874, No. 1
5. Mills' Report, Appendix J.
6. *Ibid.*
7. Bengal Govt. Resolution, dt. 19 April 1873 on Introduction of Assamese Language.
8. *Ibid.*
9. *Ibid.*
10. *Ibid.*
11. *Ibid.*
12. *Ibid.*
13. *Ibid*
14. *Ibid.*
15. A.S.F. No.1, Home A, November 1896, Nos. 142-43.
16. *Ibid*
17. *Ibid.*
18. A.S.F. No. 145G of 1881, p. 35.
19. A.S.F. No. 1, Home A, Nov. 1896, Nos. 142-43, No. 142 Edn. B 1881.
20. *Ibid.*
21. *Ibid.* No. 143.
22. A.S.F. No. Home A, December 1897, No. 50-54, Nos. 50 & 52.
23. *Ibid.*
24. A.S.F. No Home A, December, 1901, Nos. 28-32.
25. *Ibid.*, Note dated 8 June 1901.
26. A.S.F. No. Home A, August 1903, Nos. 52-57. No. 55.
27. *Ibid.*, No. 61.
28. *Ibid.*, No. 75.

29. *Ibid.*, p. 8.
30. A.S.F No. Education A, January 1914, Nos, 92-98 and Education A, March, 1929, Nos. 28-33.
31. A.S.F. No. Education A, May, 1921, Nos. 126-30.
32. *Ibid.*
33. *Ibid.*
34. A.S.F. No. Education A, March, 1929, Nos. 28-33.
35. *Ibid.*, pp. 2-3.
36. *Ibid.* No. 30.
37. A.G., 1937, Vol. VI, p. 1839-40.
38 *Ibid.*, 1937, p.123.
39. *Ibid.*, 1940, Vol. VI, pp. 1742.
40. *Ibid.* 1941, Vol. VI, pp. 364-65.
41. *Ibid.*, A.G., Vol. VI, 1948, pp. 488-89.
42. A.G. Vol. VI, 1948, pp. 581-82.

4

THE COMING OF THE ALPHABET
A Study on the Scripts of Some North-Eastern Languages

P.K. Bandyopadhyay

Languages-dialects get alphabets in two ways: one is through a process of evolution—evolution from pictograms, syllables, scripts etc.—and standardisation through printing. The other method is imposition of an alphabetic script through some social or political agencies.

The dialects of the North-Eastern India have got their scripts through the latter process. A ready made script with some additions and alterations was adopted by the Christian Missionaries. This introduction of the script brought about changes of far-reaching significance. It quickened the pace of evangelisation, education (at least 3 R's) and democratisation of reading.

It is a common-place of the study of language that many epoch-making events are just accidents of history. Whether we agree to this point of view or not, the fact remains that certain incidents take place affecting the course of the history of the life of a community. Had the Baptist Mission from Serampore not gone back from the Khasi Hills and persisted despite the initial odds, who knows whether Romanisation by the Welsh Presbyterian Mission would have been possible at all?

To elucidate the point made in the beginning, broadly two factors determine the choice and character of the scripts of a particular language group. One is the material circumstances and the other social circumstances. By 'material circumstances' we mean the nature of the surface (like the stone clay, ivory, parchment, paper, etc.) and the nature of implements (like wood-block, brush, chisel, etc.) used for transcription. By 'social circumstances' we mean the whole gamut of social, political and religious influences and factors like the range of sounds a community actually uses at the time of getting its scripts. So far as the dialects of the North Eastern Hill areas are concerned, the first factor is virtually irrelevant. Except some very rudimentary instances here and there (like the use by the Khasis of some crude forms of geometrical figures for business transactions) there was no system of transcription prevalent among these pre-literate communities. The most dominant social factor influencing the choice of script here is the "missionary enterprises". There are examples galore where imposition of scripts is the direct result of conquests, political or religious or both. In this respect, the Christian missionaries are not the solitary agents. It is true of Islam as well. Islam has forced the Arabic script on so many languages like Swahili, Malay with a phonetic system different from Arabic. Even the Pali script of the Siamese language can be attributed to the expansion of the early Indian travellers.

Coming back to the North East Indian scene, one is inclined to ascribe the Romanisation to the interest and the convenience of the Welsh Christian missionaries. There is also the view that the Roman script is more suitable to some of the dialects of the area.

> "... the Bengali script was not suitable for Khasi language, and the Roman alphabet is its more legible and simple type was found to be convenient." (Hamlet Bareh: *The Language and Literature of Meghalaya).*

The proposition is not quite tenable from the linguistic point of view. When an alien script, be it Ko-kho or Roman or Nagri or Arabic is being imposed on the dialect of a pre-literate community, the existing alphabet of the script has to be adopted with certain additions, alterations and modifications keeping in view the range of sounds of the concerned spoken languages. To be specific, Nagri which accommodates the widest possible sound range is quite capable of transliterating the Khasi language. It is, in fact, the convenience in evangelization which weighed more with the Welsh missionaries rather than considerations of suitability or otherwise of the Roman characters to the phonetic structure.

Let us have a look at the history. As stated earlier the Khasis had no script of their own. Two stories on this are current. One says that the Khasis had a script, but it was lost in a fire at *Nongkseh* and *Madur Maskut*. The other story says that at the time of flood when the Khasi was swimming away along with the script, he swallowed it finding no alternative to save it. Thus the script was lost. In the absence of any historical proof we need not take the fiction seriously.

The Serampore Baptist Mission under the leadership of Sri K.C. Pal was the first mission to come to the Khasi Hills around 1812-13. The Mission started evangelization and worked for some time. The "Gospel of St. Mathew" was translated obviously in the Bengali alphabet. William Carey took keen interest and took up the job of translation of the *New Testament*. The *Khashee New Testament* was published in 1831 in the Bengali script. A copy of the same has been kept in the Serampore College Library. Mr. Alexander B. Lish also wrote a few books and the first article on the Khasis.

The work of the Baptist was shortlived. It was the Welsh Prebyterian Mission which laid a firm base of Christianity in the Khasi Hills. The name of Rev. Thomas Jones, one of the pioneering missionaries who came to the Khasi Hills in 1841 will be written in red letters. He adopted the Roman script for the Khasi language. School books, translations from the Bible were being written in that script only. This marked a significant watershed. The reason why Rev. Jones introduced the Roman script is not far to seek. He and his missionaries were conversant with that script only and with a view to carrying on the proselytisation work without any delay they discarded the Bengali script in favour of the Roman. There were misgivings about the wisdom of the change-over even among some of the Welsh missionaries. Mr. W.J. Allen in his *Report* on the *Administration of the Cassyah* and *Jynteah Hills* Territory wrote: "Mr. W. Robinson, the Inspector of Schools and Mr. Principal

Assistant Commissioner Hudson ... are disposed to attribute the unfavourable results of these experiments in a great measure, to the use of the Cassyah language and the Roman characters in these institutions (Allen: *Report on the Administration of the Cassyah and Jynteah Hills Territory,* Article 150). But the Roman script gradually entrenched itself. Facilities in printing further consolidated its position.

However, the mode of spelling and transliteration by the Welsh Missionaries during the early period came under severe attack by some of the eminent Khasis. Mr. Hormu Rai Diengdoh, Editor of *U Khasi Mynta* rendered a detailed account in his letter to the Editor of the *Bengalee*. Calcutta on 24-9-1902. In June 1884, Mr. Charles Elliot, Chief Commissioner of Assam wrote "Not only are all the Khasi religious and educational books printed in the Roman character but the transliteration is so barbarous and uncouth that it requires the reader to learn Welsh in order to know how the words are meant to be pronounced." The Editor of *U Khasi Mynta* continued : "But we are glad now that all the independent and enlightened Khasis, the Khasi authors, the German Missionaries and other leaders of other sects and communities in Khasi have adopted a new and phonetic mode of spelling..., a spelling which is going to a right direction...."

A few examples given below will illustrate the point :

Revised spelling	*Early Welsh spelling*
Ho-oid	H'oid
Rwa'i	Riwai
Hynniew	Hiniew
Jrong	Jerong
Ryntih	Rynti

The early Welsh spelling sparked off protest from some enlightened sections of the Khasis. The name of Sri Radhon Singh Berry may be mentioned in this regard. He, in fact, suggested the revised method of spelling. Later the Welsh Missionaries also switched on to the revised method of spelling. Letters like ñ., ĩ , were added to the alphabet. After all these changes the present standardised Khasi alphabet consist of 23 letters:

A, B, K, D, E, G, NG, Ï, H, I, J, L,
M, N, Ñ, O, P, R, S, T, U, W, Y

'G' is pronounced 'eg'. In fact the English 'G' sound is not used in Khasi except to indicate non-Khasi names like Gujarat, Gauhati, etc.

Even after standardization convenience and facilities in typing and printing influence the spelling pattern. Some examples are given below:

Conservative spelling	*Modified spelling preferred by some writers*
ïng	ïng, iing
ïaid	iaid

The exact spelling of 'Syiem' (modern) according to the sound should have been Sïem, but convenience made it *Syiem* and sometimes even *Siem*. Similarly, *bayn* had become *ba'n* and then *ban*. Except words like *ia* and *ïa* where *ï* and *i* cannot be interchanged without change in meaning the votaries of the modified spelling plead for simplification.

It is thus the phonetic structure which influenced the alphabet; to transliterate certain sounds, certain new letters were also adopted. But after standardization the same alphabet turns out to be a conservative force and the speech group is more or less, required to conform to the uniform pattern. This two-way influence is a significant character of a living language.

Garo

The story of the script to the Garo language is somewhat similar to that of the Khasi. The Bengali script had been in use for more than three decades. The translation of the "Gospel by St. Mathew" published in 1875, which was followed by four Gospels in 1876 was written in the Bengali alphabet. The *New Testament* and *Old*

Testament were also rendered into Garo in the *Bengali* character. Towards the last decade of the nineteenth century, the American Baptist Mission decided to switch over to the Roman alphabet. In addition to the use of the Roman characters for new books, Romanisation of the existing translation also started on vigorous scale. Mr. E.G. Phillips, who took over the work from Mr. T.J. Keith, continued developing the Garo language in the Roman script. His early publication in the Roman alphabet included 'Anchihgnikam' in 1902. The Gospels were Romanised. The Romanisation of the *New Testament* 'Niam Kitab' was a landmark in the transliteration.

The present standardized Garo alphabet consists of the following 20 letters :

A, B, C, D, E, G, H, I, J, K, L, M, N, O, P, R, S, T, U, W
('C' is almost invariably followed by 'H')

Mizo

The Mizo language or 'Duhlian Tawng' also had no script of its own. The pioneering missionaries of the London Baptist Mission. Rev. Savidge and Lorraine who started work in 1894 A.D. in the Lushai Hills adopted the Roman script for the dialect. And that was the first script given to it. Like the Khasi story there was also a story regarding the 'Mizo script'. It says that the alphabet was written on a piece of skin. It was eaten by a dog and thus the script was lost. A good story but poor history. Evangelization was the prime motive in the introduction of the Roman script.

The present standardized Mizo alphabet consists of 25 letters:

A, AW, B, CH, D, E, F, G, NG, H, I, J,
K, L, M, N, O, P, R, S, T, **T**, U, V, Z

Arunachal Scene

Arunachal is a land of myriad dialects and tribes. Around 70 dialects are spoken. None of these except 'Khampti' had any script.

'Khampti' used a script called 'Shan' script. When the Union Territory Government abolished dialects as the medium of instruction at the Primary level in 1974, and made English the medium, the importance of dialects diminished to a great extent. There are, however, some schools where Hindi is the medium. Scholars and the Philological section of the Research Department of the N.E.F.A. (now Arunachal) Government took up the job of preparation of language-guides for various dialects mostly for officers serving in the area. These scholars used three different scripts—Nagri, Roman and Phonetic. The aim is to evolve a convenient system for practical use. But in the absence of any literary activities in the dialects and the new medium of instruction, development of the dialects is at a low ebb. The All India Radio specially the AIR Dibrugarh station has selected a few prominent dialects for broadcast of rural and cultural programmes. There is no unanimity about the choice of script and the position is likely to remain so at least in the near future.

REFERENCES

Garo Dictionary by D.S. Nengminza.

Garo Grammar by D.S. Nengminza.

Introduction to the Khasi English Dictionary by E. Bars.

Ka Jingsdang Ka Jingspel Bad Jingthoh Ia Ka Ktien Khasi Da Ki Dak Roman by U Kynpham Singh

The Khasi Canvas by J.N. Chowdhury.

Linguistic Survey of India by G.A. Grierson.

The Language and Literature of Meghalaya by Hamlet Barch.

Lusei Grammar by R. Buchhawna.

The Loom of Language by Frederick Bodmar.

Lushai English Dictionary by Rev. Savidge and Lorraine.

The Missionaries among the Khasis by Nalini Natarajan.

The Mizos by L.B. Thanga.

Report on the Administration of the Cossyah and Jynteah Hills Territory by W.J. Allen.

5

TREND OF THE LANGUAGE AND CULTURE OF MANIPUR

E. Nilakanta Singh

Manipur has an area of 8,456 square miles of which the hills surrounding the valley at the centre cover nearly 7,806 square miles. The central valley of about 700 square miles is the abode of the largest and the advanced community known as the Manipuris, or technically speaking, the Meiteis. According to the census of 1971, of the total population of Manipur (10,72,753), the tribals number 3,34,466 whereas the total number of Manipuri speaking people is about 6,38,287. The present population is likely to go up to at least 1.2 million. The Manipuri Muslims (80 thousand), Chakpas, Lois (scheduled caste Manipuris) also speak Manipuri. The number of scheduled tribes speaking various languages is 29, of which the major groups are Kabui, Mao and Tangkhul (under the Naga group) and Hmar, Paite, Thadoil, Vaiphei and Zou (broadly under what is known as Kuki group) even though the latter groups are not happy with the term *Kuki.*

Of these groups in Manipur, only the Meiteis have their own script (as against the existing Assamese-Bengali script) and an incredibly rich old literature spreads out over thousands of old manuscripts. According to the *Royal Chronicle,* the Meiteis claim their descent from King Pakhangba of 33 A.D. Leaving aside the controversial question of *Mahabharata* Manipur is identified with the present Manipur. But it is on record that there were many principalities of different groups of people speaking different tongues independent of each other. These groups or clans are: Meitei, Angom, Khuman, Luwang, Moirang, Khaaba-Ngaanba, Chenki-Sarang-Leisangthem. It is likely that from about eighteenth Century A.D. the Meiteis got the upper hand and succeeded in naming the land as that of the Meiteis (Meitrabak) which came to be known later, among themselves, as Manipur. It is also likely that as this north-eastern area was very much in the Tantric belt of India, this area corresponding to *Manipur Chakra* of the Kundalini, might be known as Manipur in the *Mahabharata* period. There is considerable evidence of the Shaivite and Tantric cult in the pre-Vaishnavite culture of the valley, as recorded in various old manuscripts, incantation and prayers of the Meitei priests which are still prevalent among the people.

The Meiteis belong to the Mongoloid people and what was known as the Kirata in the *Mahabharata* period. Under the term *Kirata* there are also other peoples like Khasi, Bodo, Kuki and others speaking allied dialects. Linguistically speaking, Manipuri or *Meitei* belongs to Tibeto-Burman group of languages (Kuki-Chin), of which the speakers are believed to have come down from the North-West of China and got themselves scattered throughout South-East Asia and entered Assam along the Brahmaputra river. The valley Meiteis have, of course, been exposed to various waves of culture from all directions—east, north, south and west. The Brahmins started arriving from all parts of India, right from fifteenth Century A.D. and got themselves merged. So is the case with Chinese, Burmese, Shans and Tais—all of which led to a composite racial group known as the *Meiteis,* as distinguished from the surrounding population of Tibeto-Burman speakers which remain as the scheduled tribes. The supreme flowering of Vaishnavite culture with *rasleela* and thousands of *Nata Mandaps* in the villages of the valley is too well known to need any introduction. It began from fifteenth Century A.D. and found supreme expression during the reign of Rajarishi Bhagyachandra (1763-1798 A.D.) in the eighteenth century.

It would now be evident that the fate of the valley in the matter of survival and growth is now linked with the outlook of the Hills people of Manipur. It is not enough that the Meiteis of the valley survive with strength and glory. The 29 tribes of Manipur have an equal claim on the resources and privileges of the entire state and they have to stand or fall together with the Hindus of the valley. Unfortunately, religion divided the people. Vaishnavism which was originally a liberating force in Bengal, became orthodox and rigid in the brahminical framework with the spirit of touch-me-notism. The tribal brethren became untouchables in their eyes and the Muslims were not allowed entry in the ordinary Meitei house. This is, indeed, a historical mistake on the part of the valley Hindus, which the people of the Hills have not been able to forget even now. This is a wound in the social fabric which does not admit of easy healing.

It is also not true that the tribals of Manipur present an integrated group. The old classification of the Manipuri tribals into Naga and Kuki is no longer tenable and is rather over-simplified. Though *Zemi-Rongmei Langmei* (known as Kabuis) and *Thadou-Paite-Hmar* share many dialectical and cultural features in common, there are many contrasting traits also. The objectives of Paite National Council (of Churachandpur) has many dissimilar aspects as against the frame of reference of the *Zelcriangrong* (of Tamenglong). There are differences, no doubt, on the tribal and even village level amongst them. But there are also some common elements shared by them: shifting cultivation, allegiance to animism or Christianity (a modern phase), presence of bachelors' dormitory (in the case of non-Christians), small bi-clan or multi-clan villages, typical dress for each group and a general consciousness of belongingness to a tribe. The Hindu Manipuris also retain something of their tribal customs: worship of household deities like *Sanamahi* and *Laimaren,* holding of annual *Lai-Haraoba* festivals before the forest or clan deities (numbering more than 300) ritual authority of the lineage Chief *Piba* and affiliation to 7 clan of *salais.*

As a matter of fact, an active group of social workers under the name 'Manipur Cultural Integration Conference' has been investigating the possibility of a common origin of the people of the hills and valley of Manipur. This is primarily an anthropological undertaking, representing at the same time a quest for identity on the part of the people of Manipur. This group has been undertaking a series of surveys to add an economic dimension to the problem and has got a few good reports to its credit. This is indeed, a commendable work. But in the eyes of the people of the hills, it looks like a political strategy, and does not get the response it richly deserves from the tribal people. This proves how deep the chasm has been between the people of the hills and the valley. Much against the wishes of the brahmins, the conference has been advocating inter-marriage which is rather an exception than the rule. But Christianity somehow stands in the way and so also politics of the land. The cry for integration, not the integration of the hills and valley of Manipur, but the integration of the areas of Manipur with Nagaland and of the areas of Manipur South with Mizoram, finds a ready response and despite the well-meaning efforts of the integrationists and social workers in Manipur, the Hill is hill and the Valley is valley and never the twain are likely to meet at least for some time to come.

Even among the valley people, there has been a tendency for disintegration. In their quest for identity and meaning, certain groups of the Meiteis discover their roots in the pre-Vaishnavite Meitei religion and refuse to call themselves Hindus. They style themselves as worshippers of *Pakhangba, Sanamahi* and *Apokpa* (forefathers) and introduce themselves as Meiteis — pure and simple. This is revivalism with a vengeance. By their persistent propaganda and anti-Hindu campaign among the people, they have succeeded in abolishing even *Puja* for the students in the schools and colleges on the plea of secularism and getting the old Meitei script recognised recently by the Government for the purpose of introduction in the schools. The idea is to replace increasingly the existing Assamese-Bengali script by the old script. What is more, they have started to remove '*Singh*' from their names and call the land Meitrabak, in place of Manipur. As a result, the people of the valley now stand divided on the level of religion and in the name of the discovery of racial roots. These are some of the disintegrating forces which divide the people of this land, and for that matter, the

Indians of this north-east corner of the country. This is Hindu *versus* Meitei, Bengali script *versus* Meitei script and even Indian versus non-Indians. It stands almost like an anti-thesis to the earlier thesis of Hindu Manipuris who were proud of their religion and culture based on the Vedic tradition. The synthesis is yet to arrive.

Even though Manipuri or Meitei is the state language of Manipur, used practically for all purposes of administration in the hills and valley of Manipur, the hills people, at least the elites of the hills, are still opposed to the acceptance of Meitei language, which is rather Sanskritised to some extent and has developed remarkable literary prose. As all the hill dialects have adopted Roman script for their developing literature, the hills people are opposed to the Assamese-Bengali script which is being used for all the modern books in Manipuri. The threat of adopting the old Meitei script would further alienate the people of the hills. It appears to be the considered view of many of the hill leaders of Manipur that uniform adoption of Roman script for all the dialects and Meitei language would be a most welcome step and once this step has been taken, they would be prepared to accept even Manipuri as the undisputed state language of Manipur. But this is a far cry from the revivalist trend of the valley people who would find it impossible to adopt the Roman script at the moment. This consideration calls for statesmanship of a high order among the leaders and supreme concern for the integration of the hills and the valley of Manipur, which is unfortunately lacking at the moment.

It is also not a fact that the tribals of the hills of Manipur are still basically tribal and primitive. The basic sense of tribalness is increasingly substituted by a generic term 'Scheduled Tribe' or *Adivasi* at least on the political plane. The two forces of Christianity and urbanisation (of the rural folks) have undoubtedly brought about a change in their world view. Their world view is now determined by concepts like exploitation/co-operation, poverty/plenty, illiteracy/education and community nation. There is now increasing modernisation of the tribal society of Manipur. There is also the phenomenon of the peasantisation of the tribes of the urban areas of Manipur, with some of their customs and beliefs being retained, besides the modernising force of education. The situation is worse in the valley. Dictated by a sense of economic frustration and increasing unemployment among the educated youths of the valley and persistent feeling of being second class citizens of India, some of the youths of Manipur have now decided to discover their tribal roots by adopting anti-Hindu attitude and adopt an extreme path in an attempt to carve out their destiny which is not linked with that of India. This is a dangerous move as is evident in the recent operation of guerilla tactics of hit and run adopted by the Communist China-trained revolutionaries under the name of PLA (People's Liberation Army). Their number is not great but it is enough to create terror among the people and the government. This is politics which represents the expression of economic frustration of a sizeable section of the youth of the valley of Manipur. This is also a warning which we can ignore at our own peril.

In the context of the alarming change in thinking and beliefs of the people, it is difficult to conceive of an integration of the hills and valley people on the basis of the common Mongoloid roots or of a common script. Awareness of a common destiny of Manipur might have a sobering effect for a while. But the forces of disintegration are also powerful. Education may perhaps point to a way of integration—education which raises the people beyond the level of religion, tradition and even languages and which quickens the pace of modernisation of the valley and the hills of Manipur. The awareness of a linguistic affinity is no solution. Linguistic identity is out of the question. The creation of a classless society, at least the efforts of establishing a socialistic culture free from exploitation and domination, appears to be the solution on the economic level. The awareness of a common destiny and of ethnic identity and roots and memories of a living together for centuries, despite the past acts of exploitation might help in the process of the integration of the hills and the valley, but not at the cost of the dream of a classless society. Economic integration at the grassroots level is the main key to the solution of the problem of Manipur: Prevention of exploitation of man by man and the flow of development benefits to the people of the hills and valley of

Manipur. Others like adoption of a common script or awareness of linguistic affinity are subsidiary to it. Economics, not languages, is the key and poverty, not ethnic identity, is the issue, and a classless society and socialist culture are the solution for the problem of the valley of Manipur.

6

LANGUAGE PROBLEM IN THE NORTH-EAST REGION

B.N. Talukdar

The language problem in the North-East is no doubt baffling and complex. But, given the will and determination, all problems however baffling and complex they may be, can be solved to the satisfaction and benefit of all. The North-eastern region is a land of about 20 million people drawn from various ethnic stocks. The number of tribes in the region is estimated to be well over 130. Each tribe speaks a different language which is not understood even by its immediate neighbouring tribe. As for instance, Arunachal Pradesh with a population of nearly half a million, speaks 50 languages. The number of tribes is estimated to be 70 within Arunachal alone. Similarly in Nagaland one tribe does not follow the language of another tribe. The A.I.R. broadcasts programme in at least 13 tribal languages for Nagaland. The population of Nagaland is almost same as that of Arunachal, Mizoram, Tripura, Manipur, Assam, Meghalaya and are all multilingual in composition and character. In such a situation to venture to offer a ready made and all acceptable solution off the sleeve will certainly look overambitious, if not ridiculous. The solution needs a careful study of the situation and the needs and aspirations of the people inhabiting the region from time immemorial. A solution tried to be imposed from outside the region is also very often looked upon with fear and suspicion. Therefore, the matter may best be left with the people depending solely on their collective wisdom to find out the best possible answer to the otherwise vexed and complex problem of language in the region.

It can, however, be pointed out that the problem of language is nothing new to the region. It existed before also. But thanks to the collective wisdom of the people that they could find out at least a workable solution and carry out the normal activities of trade and commerce, administration education and their day-to-day activities as effectively as possible under such a situation. In the process, the society slowly and steadily, with increased realisation and also under the compulsion of living together for mutual benefit and progress, gradually emerged as a multilingual society. In this process, Arunachal and Nagaland developed a language of their own which is now termed as Nagamese and Arunachalese, a kind of Assamese which is understood by different tribes speaking different languages there. This newly developed Assamese language is a kind of linguafranca for the people of the said region. The Assembly proceedings of both Nagaland and Arunachal are carried on in this language which they themselves have developed collectively and also satisfactorily. Now attempts are afoot to codify this new variety of this type of Assamese language prevalent in that part of the region. This is one instance to show how a language grows out of a necessity and how it functions effectively and satisfactorily to meet the local needs and aspiration of a people. It also illustrates a point of linguistic importance that the prescriptive grammar cannot keep a language in an iron jacket for all time to come. It changes, it grows, it expands and serves the people in removing the communication gap. But a point here needs to be stressed that while Nagaland and Arunachal have evolved a workable solution of this type, other areas like Mizoram, Meghalaya, Manipur and Tripura are yet to evolve a common and acceptable indigenous system of communication. These areas are generally dependent on English. English is used in legislature, administration and in different tribal speeches in day to day activities like trade and commerce. Sometimes, a kind of Hindi is also used in a restricted domain. But it cannot be said that people are not communicating amongst themselves. They do. In this process the society also tends to become multilingual. It is now seen a man of the region uses at least three to four languages in his day-to-day activities. A man speaks another in his field of work, viz. office, markets, educational institutions and yet another while communicating to a person or group of persons of another speech community. The way of life and the nature of work of a person normally decides the number of languages one will have to choose to carry out his normal functions in life. Therefore, we find a person say in Manipur, using Bengali at home, Meitei outside home, English in office, Hindi in market and so on. This pattern may be more or less similar in other parts of the region with slight changes of one or two languages depending on the area of operation of the person concerned.

In Assam the situation is a little different. Assamese is the state language in the state level. But in the district of Cachar, Bengali is the official language at the district level. Similarly in Karbi Anglong and North Cachar districts, people of the districts can use their own languages at the district level. In the Legislative Assembly of Assam, English, Assamese, Bengali and also Hindi are used and members generally follow the language without the help of translation. The nature of a multilingual situation perhaps is best illustrated in this case.

Now it is seen that the administration at different levels uses different languages in different parts. The medium of instruction also varies at different levels in different places. But at the higher stage of education and also at a common regional forum like North Eastern Council or national forum like the Parliament, English is the language for the people of the region. The knowledge of English, and preferably better English, thus becomes imperative for the entire region. The urge for retention of English particularly in the tribal zones, therefore, is more pronounced today. There has been a talk of replacing English by Hindi at the National level in certain quarters but this has not so far found favour on an all-India basis. The situation is likely to continue in the same fashion for the foreseeable future.

In such a situation, therefore, the region cannot turn itself to a unilingual zone at once. It will have to remain multilingual in character and composition. It is, therefore, imperative on the part of the authorities at different levels to make necessary arrangements to offer language learning facilities to the people depending on the needs and choices of the different parts of the region. There cannot be any question of imposing languages of a group or a community over that of the other. The immediate need, however, for the region is to extend the teaching and learning facilities of languages as extensively as possible. The people should be left free to choose his or her language or group of languages according to their own choice and necessity. With such an understanding and appreciation of the situation that obtains today in the region, perhaps we can delink the problem of language from politics. Nowhere politics has solved the problem of languages. The problem of language is not regional or national but universal in character. In Russia or U.S.A. or in Europe this problem does exist but the problem has been eased to a considerable extent by the collective wisdom of the people and mutual appreciation. There is, therefore, no room for any despondency that the language problem of the region cannot be solved. It can be solved. Given the will and determination, the people of the region can certainly find out the mutually acceptable solution *without,* and I stress here, *without* the advice and inducement of the politicians who are very often found to be guided by certain other interests than the cause of the language.

The demand of the languages will increase considerably now with the launching of adult education programme in a massive way. The situation and the demand can be met effectively only with a planned programme of setting up language learning centres within easy reach of the people. The success of this programme depends on the urgent attention of the authorities concerned. The three Universities of the region, Dibrugarh, Gauhati and North-Eastern Hill University have also a special responsibility in meeting the present situation.

PART – II

LANGUAGE, CULTURE AND SOCIETY

7

KINSHIP AND LANGUAGE
An Exploration of Sapir-Whorf Hypothesis in the Garo Language

D.N. Majumdar

Theoretical Perspective

Sapir and Whorf tried to find out the exact link between language and culture. Hockett explored the possibility of finding the exact link between the Chinese language and the Chinese culture (Hoijer, 1954). But he ended in a blind alley. Everybody will have to agree that a language is meaningful in the cultural context only because that particular language has grown up within that culture only, and the language serves the purpose of the bearers of that particular culture only. For example, the language must have terms for all the material objects which exist in that particular culture. The language must have concepts for all the non-material ideas with which the culture normally deals. Thus a culture which traditionally uses a hoe must have a term for it. A culture which has a belief in ghosts and spirits must have terms to distinguish these from other such phenomena. These propositions are something like axioms, because these are self-evident. Beyond these propositions it is very difficult to determine how a language and the culture of its speakers interact with each other. Some linguistic peculiarities cannot be explained as impressions of the culture on it. For example the existence of grammatical gender both in Khasi and Hindi cannot be explained by any fact in their respective cultures. We cannot say that Khasi has grammatical gender because they have matriliny. The Hindi speakers have no trace of matriliny in their culture or cultures. The present author (Majumdar, 1973) tried to correlate the peculiarity of numerical affixes in the languages of North East India to the respective cultures. It has been seen that linguistic peculiarity is present in some languages and absent in some other languages even of the same linguistic families and spoken by groups, closely akin to each other in other aspects of culture. No fact in the cultures can be adduced to explain the presence in profusion of numerical affixes in some languages. However, sometimes such linguistic peculiarities can be explained as borrowings. Thus Kakati (1941) thinks that profusion of numerical affixes in Assamese is due to the influence of the Bodo languages, because probably Assamese absorbed a section of Bodo speakers who introduced this peculiarity from their original language or languages. But again this kind of borrowing has no relationship with the cultures of the borrowers and the givers. It is worth noting that the numerical affixes in Assamese are of Indo-Aryan origin and not of Bodo origin. Considering the size and shape of the articles in counting it is certainly not a cultural factor, rather it can be regarded as a psychological factor. Though the Sapir-Whorf hypothesis emphasizes the role of language in the process of thinking, but as Peter Trudgill (1974) has pointed out, the effect of society and environment on language is more apparent.

The only direct link between a language and a culture (rather the social usages of a culture) is the kinship terminology. Kinship terminology is a linguistic phenomenon which is entirely determined by the social usages. Trudgill (1974) has also asserted this. Thus in a society where there is the practice of marrying the mother's brother's daughter it can naturally be assumed that she will not be addressed or referred to as a sister (provided, of course, that in that society there is no custom of marrying the sister also). They will have terms for all those kins who are significant and they will have no terms for those relations who are considered by the members of the society to be insignificant. If it is necessary to distinguish between two persons of the same generation, they will have two distinct terms, but if it is not necessary to distinguish in this way they will have only one term. If it is thought desirable to show deference to the seniors of the same generation there will be distinct terms to differentiate the seniors from the juniors of the same generation. However, it cannot absolutely be said that social usages entirely determine the kinship terminology. Sometimes kinship terminology can also guide social usage. For example, if in a particular terminology a particular kin is referred to or addressed as a sister, it is natural that the behaviour pattern with her will also be that appropriate for a sister. With a little introspection we will know how often we reason like this: "I call her 'sister'. How shall I marry her?" The following criteria of distinction devised by Kroebar and Lowie (1929) show distinctly what kind of distinctions may be culturally determined in a kinship terminology:

> (1) generation, (2) sex, (3) affinity, (4) collaterality, (5) bifurcation, (6) polarity, (7) relative age, (8) speaker's sex, (9) decadence.

In fact these nine criteria are the essential elements in tracing out the relationship between kinship terminology and social usages.

Within the above theoretical framework an attempt will be made here to trace out the relationship between Garo kinship terminology and Garo social usages.

Ethnographic Background

As our aim is to show the relationship between kinship and social usages, so before coming to the details of the kinship terminology it will be worthwhile to give a brief account of the Garo society, because to understand the kinship terminology it is necessary to know the society.

The homeland of the Garos is the two districts of Garo Hills in the western part of Meghalaya. According to 1971 census, Garos in two districts of Garo Hills number 3,04,864, which is 74.97% of the total population of the two districts. In Garo society descent is traced through the mother. Thus every individual is a member of one of the about 150 clans, which are matrilineal and exogamous.

The clans are primarily classified into two groups, each of these groups is also exogamous. A Garo family may be nuclear or extended matrilocal. A family usually starts as nuclear and then passes through an extended matrilocal phase and ultimately reverts to the nuclear phase. In a Garo family the usual members are a couple, their unmarried offsprings and one of the married daughters with her husband and married offsprings. The married daughter living permanently with the parents after marriage inherits all property of the household. Besides the inheritress-daughter, other daughters also may stay temporarily in the parental household but they establish nuclear families preferably in the village of the wife, within a year or so. For the daughter of the family who will inherit the property MBD type of cross cousin marriage is obligatory. For the other daughters there is no obligation, only that they should observe the rule of clan and group exogamy.

In Garo society the mother's brother plays an important part as regards marriage and conjugal lives of his sister's sons and daughters. In Garo society though a distinct trend of matriliny is present so far as descent and inheritance are concerned, we cannot say that matriarchy prevails among them, in Bachofen's sense, because women occupy a distinctly lower position in the society (Goswami and Majumdar, 1972) and affairs of the household are controlled by the male head and the affairs of the larger kin groups (i.e. lineages or clans) are controlled by the elderly male members.

A Garo marries his wife's younger sister (or somebody standing in that relationship to his wife) after the death or separation from his wife. Similar custom prevails for the females also, because they are supposed to marry the deceased husband's younger brother (or somebody standing in that relationship to her husband) after the death of her husband. Polygyny was prevalent in traditional Garo society. There was no prohibition against sororal polygyny and it was obligatory for a man to take his second (or third or subsequent) wife from his first wife's lineage (or clan). There is no trace of polyandry among the Garos. Rather it is strictly prohibited for married female to have any sort of sexual relation with any person other than her husband.

Now in the following paragraphs the Garo kinship terms will be discussed under certain broad categories. For the facility of understanding, the kin-suffixes will be omitted though in the Garo language no kinship term can be used (except in case of address) without an appropriate kin-suffix. These kinship suffixes are two in number—*tang* and *gipa*— some term taking the *tang* suffix and some others taking the *gipa* suffix. However, very often these two suffixes are used indiscriminately. In transcribing the Garo terms the standard spelling of the Garo language has been used. Kinship relations will be indicated in abbreviated form by the first two letters of the English kinship terms and "y" standing for younger and "e" standing for elder. For example, Mo-eSi—Mother's elder sister; Hu-yBr—husband's younger brother, and so on.

Kinship Terms within the Nuclear Family

In the nuclear family though descent is traced through the mother, the role of the father in the birth of the progeny is clearly recognized as also the supreme position of the father is clear; so, they have two terms *pa* (Fa) and *ma* (Mo). There is a common term to indicate offsprings, male or female. This term is *de* (So/Da) but they can particularize a son by suffixing *pante* (which when standing alone means a bachelor, but when suffixed to *de*, i.e. *depante*, the whole formation means son, married or unmarried) and also particularize a daughter by suffixing *mechik* (female). Younger siblings are expected to show respect to elder siblings, and Garos have distinct terms for elder and younger siblings, *ada* (eBr), *abi* (eSi), *no* (ySi), *jong* (yBr). There are two distinct terms *se* (Hu) and *jik* (Wi). However, the husband and the wife address each other tecnonymously when they have offsprings. In polygynous families two distinct terms are found, *jik-mongma* (wife-elephant, i.e. big wife) or *jik-mamong* (wife-principal) for the first wife who holds a superior and *jik-gite* (wife-like) for the second and subsequent wives, whose position is distinctly inferior, standing more or less in the status of concubines. However, no distinction is made between the offsprings of the principal wife and the offsprings of the subsequent wives and hence the offspring indicating terms are also used for the offsprings of the second and subsequent wives and the sibling indicating terms are used among all the offsprings of the common father. The social significance of this is that, as will be seen in a later section, a woman does not distinguish between her own offsprings and the offsprings of her sisters and in a polygynous family the second and subsequent wives are her sisters.

Kinship Terms in the Extended Family

The extension of a family takes place on the basis of matrilocal residence; one of the daughters selected to be the inheritress stays on permanently with her parents after her marriage. There is no distinct term to distinguish the heir apparent from other daughters and the general term *nokrom* is used to particularize the heir apparent, but the same term is used to indicate her husband also. Moreover, the term *nokrom* cannot be taken as a kinship term, because this term cannot be used as a term of address and this term is never used with the kin-suffix. So, here we find that the Garo kinship terminology loses sight of one important aspect of the society. Two other important relationships within the extended family are the relationships between the son-in-law and the father-in-law and between the son-in-law and the mother-in-law. The term *obite* and *neo* are used respectively for father-in-law and mother-in-law. The term *obite* is peculiar because the kinship suffixes are never added to it though like other kinship terms it can be used as a term of address. As the custom of MBD type of cross-cousin marriage is prevalent among the Garos the term *obite* and *neo* are very often confused with the terms *mama* (Mo, Br) and *mani* (MoBrWi) even though the son-in-law may not be a sister's son of the father-in-law. The younger brothers and younger sisters of the wife are expected to be treated like younger siblings by the husband also, because the *nokrom* husband has to take their responsibility after he becomes the head of the household. However, in this respect he does not identify his own siblings with those of the wife. So, he uses the terms *jongsari* (brother + suffix indicating affinity) for WiyBr and *nosari* (sister+suffix) for WiySi. The affixation of the suffix *sari* has become necessary to make a clear distinction between a real sibling from the sibling regarded as such through affinity. This distinction is absolutely necessary because after the death or desertion of the wife a man is supposed to marry his wife's sister or some female kin standing in that relation.

Kinship terms within Social Groups Larger than the Extended Family

Among the Garos the group larger than the extended family is the corporate group of the males and females descended matrilineally and among whom blood relationship can be traced. This group is called *mahari,* though such groups have no particular names. The group of a still higher order is the clan (which is called *machong*), which is a named group of persons bearing the same clan name, which descends from the mother to the offsprings. Thus, in the *machong* though it may not be possible to trace blood relationship between the members only by the fact that all the members have the same clan name it is supposed that there exists some sort of blood relationship between the members. It is to be remembered that the *machong* is very much less corporate than the *mahari.* A group of still higher order is the *satchi* which is a group of clan members of all of which feel some sort of affinity* towards each other. The *satchi* is ideally an exogamous group but has no corporateness. In the sphere of kinship terminology no distinction is made between the *mahari* and the *machong.* So the terms of the nuclear and the extended family are also used within the *mahari* and the *machong.* Thus a person in the speaker's generation within the same clan is equated to a sibling. A person in the ascending generation within the clan is equated to mother's siblings, i.e. *mama* (MoyBr, MoeBr), *Made* (MoySi), *Majong* (MoeSi). A male equates a person in the first descending generation as sister's offsprings, *gri* (SiSo), *namchik* (SiDa) and a female equates a person in the first descending generation in her own clan with her own offsprings. This difference in attitude between a male and a female about the persons in the

---

* Here I use the term affinity in the ordinary sense of linkness.

first descending generation is due to the fact that a person regards his/her mother's sister as equivalent to the mother and usually after the mother's death one of the mother's sisters takes her place. Reciprocally, a woman of the higher generation considers a person of the lower generation within the clan as her own offspring. It is also interesting to note here that Garos clearly distinguish MoySi, from MoeSi. Moreover, the term *made* (MoySi) is very often replaced by the term *ma* while *majong* (MoeSi) is always thought to be distinct from *ma.* On the other hand all persons in the descending generation of a male within the clan are his clan mates but his own offsprings belong to another clan so, these persons in his first descending generation cannot be equated to his offsprings. But a male may equate his brother's offsprings with his own offsprings for the following reasons :

(i) In the traditional pattern of Garo villages marriages usually took place between two intermarrying clans. So my wife and my brother's wife should belong to the same clan, and so my offsprings and my brother's offsprings belong to the same clan.

(ii) My wife uses the term *e* to the children of my brother for the above reason and hence if they are her *e* they are my *de* also.

(iii) As will be explained later my brother's offsprings equate me with their MoSiHu which term is broadly equated with the term for father.

The terms used outside the clan or lineage are the terms used for affines, because females of another clan in the opposite clan group (*satchi)* are one's potential mates. Hence for a female in another clan in the opposite *satchi* is *sari* (HuSi) when in the same generational level, *mani* (MoBrWi) when in the first ascending generation. For a male another male in another clan in the opposite *satchi* is *mosa* or *boning* (WiBr) when in the same generational level and *awang* (FayBr) or *pajong* (FaeBr) when in the first ascending generation. A person of the opposite sex in another clan in the opposite *satchi,* when in the same generation, is *chame* (lover or potential spouse) and for a male a female in the first ascending generation is *mani* (MoBrWi) and for a female a male in the first ascending generation in the opposite *satchi* is *pajong* (MoeBr) or *awang* (MoyBr).

Kinship Terms in the Ascending Generations

The most important and interesting among the ascendancy terms is the term for MoBr. It has already been stated how the mother's brother plays an important function in the Garo society. But the term which is used to indicate this relationship appears to be of extraneous origin (*cf.* Assamese *mama,* Bengali *mama,* Hindi *mama,* etc. probably from Sanskrit *matua* Karve, 1953). This is enigmatic. Is there no term of Garo origin for this important kin? In the Chisak dialect of Garo we come across the term *o* which is used to indicate MoBr. It is to be marked that this term is similar to the term for WiFa, *obite,* the only difference being that the term *o* takes the kin-suffix while the term *obite* does not take it. It is also interesting to note that in Garo society a mother's brother, whether younger than the mother or older than the mother or even when younger than the speaker himself commands respect. So it is considered not necessary to make a distinction between MoyBr and MoeBr.

In Garo terms for indicating kinds in the second ascending and second descending generations are not well developed. In the type of the extended family which is found among the Garos, it would have been justified to distinguish parents of the mother (who are co-residents in the extended family) from the parents of the father (who have very little to do with the son's offsprings) as is done in many kinship terminologies of the northern zone and the central zone of India (Karve, 1953). But the Garo have only two terms, *atchu* (MoFa or FaFa) and *ambi* (MoMo or FaMo). It is interesting to note that the term *atchu* appears to be similar to the term *ajja, ajo,* etc. used in many northern Indian Indo-Aryan languages which Karve (1953:187) derives from Prakrit *ajja-a* from Sanskrit *arya.* The only other term to indicate a kin in the second ascending generation is *mama-atchu* (MoMoBr or FaMoBr, though more commonly it is used as MoMoBr) which apparently is a combination of two terms *mama* and *atchu*.

Beyond the second ascending generation the Garos have no terms to indicate a kin, because usually people have relations with the second ascending and descending generations only and not with the third as usually the third ascending generation dies out before the third descending generation comes into being.

The only term to indicate kins in the second descending generation is *su* which may mean almost anybody whether belonging to the speaker's clan or not, in the second descending generation. It is also interesting to note that the terms for the second ascending generation can also be used to indicate a person in the second descending generation. For example, *atchu* may mean FoFa, FaFa as well as SoSo or DaSo.

Terms for Spouses for Kins

In the Garo type of joint family a male has chance of coming in close contact with his wife's sisters' husbands, because they may live in the same household unit for a considerable time. But the term they use to indicate this relationship appears to be of extraneous origin. They use the term *sadu* to indicate this relationship and strangely enough this term is found in the kinship terminology of the northern zone which Dr. Karve derives from Sanskrit compound *sa (ha)-vadhuka* influenced by the secondary *Vodhrka,* those who have wives together (Karve, 1953:139). So it can be said that a term which is very much necessary in the social situation may also be lacking in the terminology. A man or a woman has the chance to be very close to his sister's (elder) husband and to indicate this relationship they have the term *gume.* On the other hand a man's relation with his younger sister's husband is different from that of a female with her younger sister's husband. For a male the younger sister's husband is *musa* or *boning* and this term is used without observing the rule of polarity. This is an important relationship in the Garo kinship matrix, because the wife's elder brother, as a senior male member of the wife's lineage has many responsibilities towards his sister's household. But the strange fact about this term is that both the terms appear to be of extraneous origin (*cf.* Goalpara dialect of Assamese where *mosai* and *bonai* are the terms to indicate this relationship. Dutta, 1971). Thus a socially significant relationship is indicated by a borrowed term, while the social peculiarity is not a borrowed one. For a female the younger sister's husband stands in the relationship of a son-in-law (because, there is likelihood that the elder female would achieve the position of head of the household at one time) and so the term *chawari* (DaHu) is used by her to indicate her younger sister's husband and the younger sister's husband uses the term *neoseksari* (neo, WiMo and *sari* a suffix to indicate generally a female affine) to indicate his wife's elder sister. There is no chance for a man to come in close contact with his male affine's wife (because both are members of different households which may stand apart from each other by a long distance). But the Garos have a term to indicate this relationship and this term is the same term as the term for SiDa (*namchik).* This is probably because in traditional Garo villages there were two intermarrying clans and as such a man's wife's brother's wife naturally belongs to the man's clan and younger in age. There is not much of relationship between a person and his/her elder brother's wife, the term *bochi* is however used to indicate this relationship, and this term also appears to be of extraneous origin (*cf.* Bengali *bodi).*

Terms for Kins through Males

Matriliny is the most important element of Garo society. As such we find that terms for kins through male are not well developed. It will not be an exaggeration to say that Garos do not have terms to indicate kins through males, and invariably kins through males are indicated by an analogy to kins through females. Thus FayBr (*awang*) = MoySiHu (*awang*); FaeBr (*pajong*)=MoeSiHu (*pajong*); HuyBr (*jongsari*)=WiyBr (*jongsari*); HuySi (*nesari*)=WiySi (*nesari*); HuFa (*odite*)= WiFa (*odite*); HuMo (*neo*)=WiMo (*neo*); FaSi (*mani*) = MoBrWi (*mani*); FaSiHu (*mama*)=MoBr (*mama*); SoWi (*namchik*)=SiDa (*namchik*); HueBr (*obite*)=WiFa (*obite*). It has been found that the term *namchik* is used in three contexts, primarily it means SiDa. But it is extended to mean SoWi, and affine's wife, WiBrDa. If in a social group MBD type of cross cousin marriage is practised from generation to generation then a man's SoWi will be his SiDa. A man's FaSi will be his MoBrWi etc. as will be seen from the following diagram :

O	Stands for male
△	Stands for female
II	Stands for marriage
- - - -	Broken lines indicate that the person is same
I	Vertical lines indicate descent.

REFERENCES

Dutta, B., 'Dialects of Goalpara District', *Assam Academic Review* (ed. B. Barua), No. 1, 1971.

Goswami, M.C. and Majumdar, D.N., *Social Institutions of the Garos of Meghalaya*, Calcutta, 1972.

Hoijer, Harry, 'The Relation of Language and Culture' in Kroebar and others. *Anthropology Today*, 1953.

Hoijer, Harry, (ed), *Language in Culture*, Univ. Chicago Press, 1954.

Kakati, Banikanta, *Assamese, Its Formation and Development*. Gauhati, 1941.

Karve, Irawati, *Kinship Organization in India*, Asian Publishing House, 1953.

Lowie, R.H., 'Relationship Terms', *Encyclopaedia Britannica*, London, 1929.

Majumdar, D.N., 'Size-Shape Categories in the Languages of North East India, An Exploration of the Sapier-Whorf Hypothesis', *Bulletin of the Department of Anthropology*, Gauhati University, Vol. II, 1973.

Mandelbaum, David G., (ed). *Selected Writings of Edward Sapir*, Berkeley, Univ. Calif. Press, 1949.

Trudgill, Peter, *Sociolinguistics: An Introduction*, Penguin Books, 1974.

Whorf, Benjamin L., *Language, Thought and Reality* (ed. John B. Carron), Mass Inst. Tech., 1953.

8

NON-STANDARD FORMS OF ASSAMESE
Their Socio-cultural Role

Birendranath Datta

I may be permitted to start this chapter with an anecdote.

A few years back a young undergraduate from Gauhati had for a short period taken up a job as a school teacher in a rather obscure and out-of-the way village in north Kamrup. A friend of his hailing from Sibsagar district came to visit him in the village and was taken to the house of a villager with whom our young teacher had struck up a friendship. After the customary exchange of courtesies, the host went inside and the two friends were for a time left along with the five-year old son of the host. In a bid to be friendly and intimate with the boy the visitor from Sibsagar, who happened to be a college graduate, started talking to him in the best Sibsagar dialect at his command. The youngster showed little sign of comprehension and soon ran into the inner apartments shouting excitedly, "Mother! Mother! These people are Bengalees," The two friends stood thoroughly aghast and scandalised.

The explanation of the queer reaction of the boy is really quite simple. The visitor from Sibsagar was speaking in a language that was strange and exotic to the youngster who had heard it spoken for the first time. As far as he was concerned, no Assamese could speak in a tone different from the one he himself spoke. As he had heard that the Bengalees spoke differently from the Assamese, the visitors got identified as Bengalees. (The same boy would certainly have reacted differently after some years, having been exposed to standard Assamese through school education.)

Now, the friends had every reason to be scandalised as they were used to the position that the Sibsagar Assamese is the standard Assamese and the other forms of Assamese are only dialects—non-standard forms of the language. And the village concerned spoke one of these.

On the other hand, there is something to be said in defence of the boy. Although in his ignorance and naivete he had confused the Sibsagar colloquial with Bengali, his reaction nevertheless highlights the truth that the Sibsagar colloquial is one of the dialects of the Assamese language and its being recognised as the standard form of Assamese in no way detracts from that truth.

And we are in good company when we say that the standard form of language is a particular dialect of that language which receives prominence and priority due to political, social, religious or other reasons and comes to be recognised and established at any particular time as the standard form and that non-standard dialects of the language are as much constituents of the language as the standard one.[1] According to E.H. Sturtevant, "A dialect which imposes itself upon the speaker of other dialects is called a standard language."[2]

And what, after all, is a dialect? According to an expert on dialectology, Raven I. McDavid, Jr., a dialect "is simply a habitual variety of a language, regional or social. It is set off from all other such habitual varieties by a unique combination of language features: words and meanings, grammatical forms, phrase structures, pronunciations, patterns of stress and intonation. No dialect is simply good or bad in itself; its prestige comes from the prestige of those who use it. But every dialect is in itself a valid instrument of human communication, and something worthy of serious study."[3] Now, in case of Assamese it is the Sibsagar dialect which has been the standard language for about two centuries. It was first given a superior status by the Ahom court and it extended practically to all parts of upper or eastern Assam under its "levelling influence". Later the missionaries made Sibsagar their centre of activities including literary activities which ushered in the modern age of

Assamese literature; and as they used the Sibsagar dialect for this purpose, the process of establishment of this dialect as the standard form of Assamese became complete.[4] The rise of a neo-aristocratic elite class in upper Assam held by the development of the tea industry might have bolstered the position of this dialect.

So much for the standard Assamese dialect. But what about the non-standard ones? Most of them are spread all over the western parts of the state comprising the Mangaldai region of Darrang district (covering the territory of the Darrang kings) in the east, Kamrup district in the middle and Goalpara district in the west. In these parts in place of the comparative uniformity in the dialectal patterns found in eastern Assam, we find variations which are both many and sharp. The reason for this has been aptly put by Dr. B. Kakati: "Western Assam was never for a long period under any dominant power. It was the cockpit of several fighting forces—the Koches, the Muhammadans and the Ahoms, and political fortunes passed from one power to another. A steady commanding influence that gives homogeneity to manners as to speech was never built up by any ruling power in western Assam."[5]

Region-wise the principal dialects of western Assam may be listed as given below:

In Kamrup:[6]

(a) Western Kamrupi-spoken in Barpeta and surrounding areas.
(b) Central Kamrupi-spoken in Nalbari region and extending upto the easternmost border of the district.
(c) Southern Kamrupi-spoken in the southern parts of the district.

In Goalpara:[7]

(a) Eastern Goalpariya-spoken in the eastern and southern portions of the district except the southern-west corner.
(b) Western Golpariya-spoken in the western-most parts of the district including the south-west corner.

(c) An intermediate dialect which is spoken in between the two regions incorporating features from the two.

In Mangaldai : Mangaldoiya-spoken practically throughout the sub-division.

Of these the Mangaldoiya dialect is closely related to Central Kamrupi; East Goalpariya has clear affinity with western Kamrupi, East Goalpariya is a variety of what Grierson called the Rajbansi dialect.

All the western dialects differ, to a greater or lesser extent, from the standard colloquial both phonologically and morphologically. There are, however, few differences in respect of basic phonemes. But as we proceed westward, the differences become categorical and more pronounced; and in the case of West Goalpariya they extend to the field of basic phonemes as well. For example, the distinctive h sound of Assamese is absent in the West Goalpariya dialect; again ṭ, ṭh, ḍ, dh and ṭ, ṭh, ḍ, ḍh retain their dental and cerebral values respectively in West Goalpariya whereas they all become alveolar in other dialects of Assamese. Similarly with c, ch and s sounds, they are present in West Goalpariya but absent in other Assamese dialects.

Ever since the establishment of the Sibsagar dialect—with its extensions in the upper Assam region as the court-patronised standard language, the lower Assam dialects had come to occupy an 'inferior' position. Coupled with the fact that the people of the lower Assam region were conquered by the Ahom at a much later stage, the different nature of their culture—characterised by their non-standard speech—set them apart from the people of the standard-speaking region. A derogatory term, *dhekeri,* was attached both to the people and their speech. The dislike of *dhekeris* at times reached such proportions that they were made to suffer indignities. On the other hand, the people of the western parts, ruled for a long time by Kamata and Koch kings, "looked upon the Narayan family as their overlords. They considered the Ahoms as outsiders...".[8] Later on this no longer remained a question of Ahom and non-Ahoms but became one of easterners and westerners, and the term *dhekeri* continued to be used as a pejorative.[9] By this, naturally the easterners did not quite endear themselves to the westerners. Such opposition obviously did not encourage communications between them. This kind of mutual distrust centring round dialectal differences is by no means rare. Instances can be cited from all over the world. The much-publicised Ghoti-Bangal maladjustment between the speakers of West Bengal and East Bengal dialects respectively is a glaring example supplied by our neighbours next door.

Fortunately the unsavoury chapter in the history of Assamese life is now practically closed. Over the years there has been a progressive change in attitudes and also in the social standing of the dialects *vis-a-vis* the standard Assamese. A consciousness has gained ground that Assamese culture is a composite culture encompassing the sub-cultures of both eastern and western Assam regions, and that as vehicles of the sub-cultures of the western Assam regions, the western Assam dialects are as important as eastern Assamese. Scholars have shown that it is rather through the western Assam dialects that the development of modern Assamese has to be traced. As such, the Kamrupi and Goalpariya dialects are no longer viewed with a feeling of contempt but with one of tolerance and even of ready acceptance. So much so that Kamrupi folksongs are today sung by upper Assam boys and girls almost as eagerly as Bihu songs by their lower Assam counterparts.

On the other hand, with the spread of education and the rapid development of the media, speakers of the western dialects are using the standard language in a more free and uninhibited manner since it has been accepted by them as the symbol of the oneness and wholeness of Assamese culture. This acceptance has been particularly conspicuous in the case of the people of the westernmost parts of Goalpara who speak a dialect substantially different from the standard one. Now that it has been established that their dialect is directly connected with modern standard Assamese through old Kamrupi whose clear traces it still retains, this acceptance has become easy. Consequently with these people who had felt only vaguely connected with "standard" Assamese culture, identification with the wider concept of Assamese culture is more or less complete. In the process there has been some amount of mutual borrowing, the non-standard dialects naturally being more on the receiving side. But the standard language itself has been undergoing certain changes what with contact with the 'non-standard' dialects and what with exposure to the media.

In recent years with Gauhati becoming the political, commercial, educational and cultural centre of Assam, there are signs of the development of a new standard dialect with an urban bias in place of the essentially rural bias of the Sibsagar dialect, which will be able to adapt itself better to the complex and fast changing socio-cultural milieu.

We have so far been dealing with regional dialects of Assamese. But there are also social dialects within each region—different ethnic or social groups within the same region forming more or less homogeneous and exclusive speech communities by virtue of peculiarities in basic vocabulary, pronunciation, intonation, and so on. For example, apart from the fact that the Muslims of Assam often use certain exclusive terms and expressions—particularly those related to religious beliefs and customs, socio-religious ceremonies like marriage, betrothal, birth, burial, and so on, and kinship terms—the language spoken by upper Assam Muslims also have some distinctive phonetic features. Exclusive kinship terms also obtain among the Ahoms. Again, the urban dialects—particularly among the middle class—are somewhat different from the rural dialects. With the growth of urbanisation, industrialisation and commercialization, newly acquired terms and expressions are fast making their entry into the middle-class urban dialects. The dialects of the adolescent and youth communities in the urban areas are very heavily loaded with exotic, hybrid and local slangs. All these merit serious study.

Students of dialectology and sociolinguistics could also study with profit the peculiar exclusive 'class dialect' current among the initiates of the Assamese Vaisnava order called *bhakats*, from which the dialects popularly known as *bhakatiya bhaha*. Characterised by a stance of extreme politeness and courtesy, the dialect leans heavily on euphemisms and makes extensive use of the passive voice and what is called *bhavvacya*, particularly in conversations. Here are a few examples:

Standard Assamese	*Literal English rendering*	*Bhakatiya bhaha*
moi bhat khalo	I have eaten rice	*saul hijoamuthi dhara ho* (Literal English rendering) The fistful of boiled rice has been got hold of.
tamol ekhan khaok/khak	Eat a piece of betel nut (prepared)	*gua edukhari betel nut bhanga jak* (Lit. Eng.) Let a piece of betel nut be broken.
Kor para ahil?	Where have you come from?	*kor para ba aha hol?* (Lit. Eng.) Where from has been the coming [I wonder]?

There is also the secret restricted language used by the pseudo-Vaisnava sect, known variously as *rati khowa, bhitarpanthiya,* etc., while performing their secret religious rites. This language is highly symbolic and metaphorical, and words and expressions often mean something very different from their ordinary connotations.

Of particular interest from the overall sociological point of view are the dialectal forms which are used by the people of the different tribal stocks living all over Assam at different levels of acculturation. In the plains there are the Bodos, the Rabhas, the Mishings, the Tiwas and others who are normally bilingual—speaking the tribal language at home and the local forms of Assamese for a outside communication. But the Assamese used by each is practically an independent dialect as it is very much influenced by the peculiarities of pronunciation, intonation, stress and accent and even vocabulary and syntax of the respective tribal languages. Thus we can say that there is *Mishing Eastern Assamese, a Bodo Central Kamrupi, a Rabha Eastern Goalpariya,* and so on. Developed as mediums of culture contact, these tribal oriented dialects have played a vital role in the welding of the diverse tribal elements into the

Assamese cultural milieu —a task a single standard Assamese or even the major regional dialects would have failed to perform. Sankaradeva the great social reformer that he was, was conscious of this functional utility of these dialects as is evidenced by an anecdote from his life as recounted in the *Kathagurucharita,* an old canonical biography. Govinda, a Garo, had become a favourite disciple of Sankaradeva. He used to address Sankaradeva as *tai,* the familiar second person pronoun normally used in addressing inferiors. Some conservative disciples took exception at this and on one occasion advised Govinda to address the saint by the polite term *tumi* or the honorific *tomra* (prevalent in the monastic Vaishnava circle), Govinda went home only to come back a few days later with some presents to see the *guru.* "So, Govinda, you are back so soon!" inquired Sankaradeva. "Yes", replied Govinda, "I have come to address you (using *tai)* as *tumi" (Toke tumi buliboloi ahilo.)* In his eagerness Govinda had somehow managed to use the word *tumi* but in effect he was still continuing to address Sankaradeva as *tai.* Now, this is exactly the character of the tribal dialect used by Govinda. Since there is a single second person pronoun to designate you in his tribal language, the Assamese dialect used by him has no three equivalents but just one—*tai,* and he meant no disrespect to his *guru* by addresssing him as *tai.* How well Sankaradeva realised this; for, his reply was, 'Govinda, I am not as pleased when others address me as *tumi* as when you call me *tai.*[10] Significantly, some of the major dialects themselves bear marks of the influence of tribal tongues— particularly at the folk levels of the society. For example, the second person pronoun *tai* is almost universally used by common people in South Kamrup and East Goalpara. Again, such pronunciations as *Khang* (I/We eat) *korlung* (I/we have done) seem to reflect a tribal tinge.

And speaking of tribal-oriented forms of non-standard Assamese we cannot but take into account the pidgin forms of the language which have for long served not only as the means of communication between the people of the hills and plains but also as the lingua franca between the various ethnic sub-groups in the hills speaking different tribal languages unintelligible to one another. The best example of such forms are Nagamese and Nefamese, in use in Nagaland and Arunachal Pradesh respectively. Basically two contact languages extending from Assamese, they have not only proved functionally useful among the people of the two regions but have also gained sufficiently respectable status to be used for formal public purposes, including radio broadcasts. Whatever their future, there is no denying the fact that they have played a historically important role.

Before conclusion, I would refer in passing to the peculiar variety or rather varieties of hybrid language spoken by the tea-garden community comprising labourers and ex-labourers, drawn from various ethnic groups, their ancestors originally coming from such far-off places as Bihar, Orissa, Madhya Pradesh, etc. Although the varieties of the language spoken by them are made of hodgepodge admixtures of Hindi, Bengali, Oriya and the languages of the original tribal groups, with more and more elements of Assamese being thrown in, they have completely identified themselves as local people and adopted Assamese as their formal standard language. With this background, it is more likely that in place of the hybrid language they now speak— which is some sort of a pidgin—a separate variety of Assamese dialect will eventually emerge among them, since these people have no extraneous cultural pulls, having lost practically all contacts with their respective original ethnic sub-cultures.

NOTES AND REFERENCES

1. See Dr. U.N. Goswami: *Bhasa Vijnan,* 1976, p.9.
2. E.H. Sturtevant : *Linguistic Change*, 1962. p. 157.
3. Raven I. McDavid, Jr. 'Sense and Nonsense about American Dialects' in *Readings in American Dialectology*, ed. H.B. Allen & G.N. Underwood. 1971. p. 42.
4. See Dr. B. Kakati. *Assamese. Its Formation and Development*, pp. 16-17. Also Dr. U.C. Goswami, *Kamrupi : A. Dialect of Assamese,* 1970. pp. 10-15.
5. Dr. B. Kakati. *Ibid.*, p. 17.

6. Dr. Kakati speaks of five dialectal regions in Kamrup (See *ibid.,p.* 17). However, Dr. U.C. Goswami who has made a comprehensive study of the Kamrupi dialect, gives the three varieties mentioned here. For detail, see, his *Kamrupi : A Dialect of Assmese,* p. 28.

7. For details see the present writer's paper, 'The Dialects of Goaplara' in *Assam Academy Review,* No. 1, 1971.

8. Dr. S.K. Bhuyan, *Anglo-Assamese Relations,* p. 271.

9. Grierson had observed that the Assamese spoken in the districts of Kamrup and Goalpara "is sometimes called *dhekeri,* which is considered more or less a term of opprobrium, having been first used when the portion of Assam, now known as Kamrup and Goalpara district, was conquered by the Ahoms....", *Liguistic Survey of India,* Vol. V, Part 1.

10. It may be noted that similarly situations are encountered in many other languages of the world. See Peter Trudgill, *Sociolinguistics: An Introduction,* 1974, pp. 105-110.

9

LOAN WORDS IN NORTH-EASTERN INDIA

P. Goswami

It has been observed that "As a community changes, there is a constant demand for new words—to express new concepts or attitudes, to denote new objects or institution, and so on"[1]. In a way, a community goes on changing all the time, learning from other contiguous communities or expanding its own activities in the fields of commerce or culture. Thus, perhaps, even the most isolated and conservative community has to borrow words to indicate new ideas or objects. In the modern world, as there has been greater contact between community and community, the tendency towards acceptance of words from the outside is more noticeable.

The situation that I have described is more or less normal, but on occasions a community may have to undergo drastic changes, as when this part of India lost its independence in the early decades of the last century. The loss of Assam's independence was sealed with the treaty of Yandabo in 1826. Soon after other contiguous areas in the hills also started losing their independence. With the coming in of non-Indian rulers, with different outlooks on administration, commerce, society and education, the dominance of local people in these fields lost its hold. Assam had led a rather isolated existence and when the Burmese invaders brought about a state of chaos, the advent of the English was accepted almost as a relief. The more alert of the people also realized the superiority of the new rulers in their organizational and administrative activities. English rule became a *fait accompli.* What was true of Assam was also true of the contiguous parts of Assam.

The judicial system that the British established brought in, amusingly, some Arabic terms, like *hākim* (magistrate), *ukil* (pleader), *ray* (verdict), *jamin* (surety), *amolā* (official), *āmol* (reign, period of administration), *khājānā* (tax), *jila* (district), dākhāl (possession). These terms had already obtained in other parts of India and served very well as equivalents to the strange English terms. The English court was served by a Hindustani term anglicised as cutchery (Assamese *Kachāri).*

It is not that independent Assam was entirely cut off from the cultural and political scense of the Hindustani world, for if one turns over the leaves of the Buranji chronicles of Assam, one comes across words like *ādmi* (Arabic-Hindustani), *sipāi* (Persian), *hārām* (Arabic), *ukil* (Arabic: in the sense of emissary), *hajir* (Arabic), *saheb* (Arabic in the sense of gentleman), *hukum* (Arabic)[2]. These terms were used in particular contexts, either in diplomatic associations or inreference to events in the Mughal world, which included Bengal, and not in order to fulfil local needs. This use indicates a sense of reality and truth in the narration of the Assamese Buranjis, written from about the end of the seventeenth century. It is to be noted that even sixteenth century Vaishnavite writers of the land used a few words of Perso-Arabic origin, for example *naphar* (servant), *pharmān* (order, fiat).

The Arabic words that became popular, and useful, after the English set-up their rule need not be traced to the Buranjis, for these documents were not meant for public consumption : their circulation was limited to the circle of high officials. Two other Arabic words found very useful were *dokan* (shop) and *banduk* (gun), the latter must have been introduced before the English came into the land. The Assamese word *hilai* usually referred to cannon; there was the necessity of a word like *banduk* to indicate something that was handy and portable.

In the field of education various English words were found indispensable. At first the *school* came, a secular institution which provided opportunity to learn the language of the new rulers; then came associated items like *master, chair, bench, slate, pencil, class,*

Sometimes two equivalent terms like class and *sreni* came to be used simultaneously and Sanskritic *sreni* has not died out even now. By and by other insitutions of instruction like college and university also came to be introduced and the names stuck. Though Iswar Chandra Vidyasagar invented the word *viswavidyalaya* about a century ago and it came to be accepted, the foreign word *university,* though not easy to pronounce, seems to be supplementing the Indian term. The college and the university have introduced terms like *principal, professor, registrar.*

With the new rulers came a new system of commerce and industry. This system popularised words like *dokan* (Arabic), *gola* (Hindustani), *namuna* (Persian), *batal* (Eng. bottle), *sah* (Hindustani chai), *kal* and *kalghar* (Hindustani-Assamese), *sardar* (Persian), *manager* (English), *Coolie* (Turkish?), *thikadar* (Hindustani). One aspect of commerce is seen in certain new items of dress that came into use. Assamese had formerly *chola,* a garment of indeterminate shape, and the word is used even now to indicate a sewn upper garment, whether it is a shirt, coat or frock, but specific items of modern dress, like *coat, pant, shirt, frock, half-pant:* all came to be a part, if I may be allowed to suggest, of the new educational system. If formerly a child ran about with just some sort of *dhoti* around his loins, he now had to go to school with a *dhoti* and a shirt or a half-pant (shorts) and a shirt. For a little girl the frock was found to be convenient to cover her upper and lower parts. Commerce certainly took a hand in encouraging these new dress items.

With the English came Marwari businessmen and Bengali assistants. Bengali and Assamese are closely related languages and at one time for several decades Bengali was even a language of the court and the school. The new Bengalee communities that settled in the large towns came to have some influence in Assamese life—in dress, food habits and social activities. The new dress items, which had already become fashionable in Calcutta or Dacca I have already mentioned. In food habits, the *rasagolla* and *sandesh* came to be accepted as attractive new sweets. Perhaps *luchi* made from fine flour was another major introduction. In social life the *barowari* or public *puja,* which had first been performed near Santipur in Bengal about in 1790, came to occupy a significant place though this sort of *puja* subsisting on public subscriptions tended to take the character of a festival rather than a religious function.

Indian languages find it easy to coin new words from Sanskrit resources, but sometimes it is less trouble if one just borrows a word from another neighbouring or familiar language. Bengali itself borrows from Hindi; similarly Assamese seems to have borrowed words like *paristhiti* (situation), *kelenkari* (scandal) replacing an earlier *khilingkar, galpa* (story), *upanyas* (novel), *prajapati* (butterfly) in spite of the local *pakhila, kusangskar* (superstition), *satabdi* (century). The useful word *natum* (Hindi?) is not found till the nineteenth century. The earlier word *na* (sans. *nava*) still exists.

A developed language as a rule is not eager to borrow words indicating abstract ideas; words associated with material objects tend to be borrowed in a larger number. A few words of the later class seem to indicate landmarks in cultural history of Assam. The *nagara,* the large kettle-drum, so closely associated with Vaishnavite music, is of Arabic origin. When was it borrowed? I have seen *nagara* even at Samarkand—the same size, the same make. The instrument must have been noticed in northern India by neo-Vaishnavite reformers in their travels. Akbar himself is said to have been an expert *nagara* player. To come to a more mundane level, Assam has a reputation for spinning and weaving. The *mako* or shuttle is a vital part of the domestic loom, but as it seems, the word is not of Assamese or even Indian origin: it is Persian. What did people do when this shuttle was not there? Did they make narrow strips of cloth on a loom tied to their waist as is seen in certain parts of eastern India? In the same manner, *chereki* (the bamboo implement for winding yarn) is also of Persian origin.

Though Assamese is basically a Sanskritic language it has been in contact with Sino-Tibetan languages for many centuries and naturally absorbed many nouns, verbs and adjectives from these languages. These loans entered the language quite early, much before the advent of the English in this region. Some non-Sanskritic loans in common use are *dao* (the large knife), *jakhala* (ladder), *tangi* (platform house to watch over crops), *khang* (anger), verbs like *selek* (lick), *gasak* (trample), *butal* (pick up), *Buranji* (history) is a reminder of the Ahom rulers' interest in recording current political events. Many river and place names in Assam have to be traced back to a non-Sanskritic origin.

I have so long spoken of loan words in Assamese, but some of the new words and concepts which came along with the English are to be found in the tribal languages as well. *School, college, pencil, pen, football, engine, pant, coat* all English; and *dokan, thikadar, jahaj, sah, gari* (vehicle) from other sources, are a few of the many words found in most languages of north-eastern India. What has struck me is that some of the tribal languages had to borrow a fair number of words indicating abstract ideas. It is seen that Khasi has had to borrow words in order to indicate happiness, sorrow, sin, time and even justice:

bāsuk (Sanskritic)	happy
bāduk (Sanskritic)	unhappy
jingshishā (Sanskritic)	truth
pāp (Sanskritic)	sin
niam (Sanskritic)	religion
bahok (Arabic)	just, honest
kahok (Arabic)	honesty
jingmap (Arabic)	forgiveness
barabor (Persian)	always
rong (Sanskritic)	colour
por (Sanskritic)	time

A few other loan words are *hikai* (teach), *dor* (price), *jubab* (reply), *dud* (milk), *jaka* (place), *khajana* (tax). These words are now handled by Khasi grammar as native elements, for instance, *hikai* may be turned into *nonghikai* (teacher), *suk* into *jingsuk* (happiness). Khasi and Assamese *dor/dar* (price) has become *dawr* in Mizo, meaning a shop or place where one gets things at a price. An important Mizo loan is *lekha* (write) which has given such combinations as *lekhatui* (ink), *lekhabu* (book).

The most significant abstract term borrowed by the Kacharis is *dhoram* (religion), from *dharam, dharam* (Sans.). Kacharis have also borrowed the word for sin—*phab* (Sans. *pap*). Other Kachari loan words are *aro* (and; Assamese *aru*), *buhur* (spirit; Assamese *bhut), dahat* (current: Assamese *dhar*). *basor* (year: Assamese basar), *Baisagu* (Assamese *Baihag— Baisakh), jonom* (Assamese *janam,* birth). Two significant words borrowed by Garo are *golpo* (story) and *git* (song), the first perhaps from Bengali and the second from Assamese.

Loan words may not be received directly from the lending languages; they often come through the medium of some intermediate language. Hindustani has been the means of circulating words of Arabic and Persian origin. Some words must have come through Bengali as well. A point to note here is that loans are not necessarily absorbed as they are in the lending languages, certain changes occur depending on the sound system of the borrowing language. For example, Sanskritic *pap* has become *phab* in Kachari; Assamese or Hindustani *dharam* has become *dohoram* in Kachari, this being an illustration of the linguistic feature anaptyxis. Similarly, English *master* and *bench* have become *mastar* and *bensi* in Assamese. *Kakat* (paper, Assamese) perhaps borrowed from Jaintia-Khasi, has by analogy become in Khasi *ka kot,* the first particle having been considered the same as the article *ka.* Medieval Hindi *kāgad (cf.)* Kabir's compositions) has become kākat (paper) in Assamese while we have in Khasi *ka-kat,* the first particle having been considered the same as the definitive *ka.*

REFERENCES

1. Charles Barber, *The Story of Language*, 1965, p. 215.
2. Hem Chandra Goswami (ed), *Purani Assam Buranji*, 1922.

10

SOCIOLOGY OF LANGUAGE
North-Eastern Case

Sudhansu S. Tunga

North-Eastern India, as we all know, is a geographical unit. It is not a society but a conglomeration of societies—each a small group of people that live and work together, have a distinct lifestyle and heritage, speak a separate language and even aspire for a separate political identity. The differences are, however, nowhere more visible than in their languages. Linguistically, the region indeed presents the maximum diversity, with more than 50 languages altogether, excluding Assamese and Bengali. The area is small, covering barely 9 per cent of the country and, therefore, has the largest concentration of languages in India. Total number of speakers in them is in the range of 2.5 million and constitutes less than 0.5 per cent of the total population of the country. Naturally the liguistic groups are small, so small that none of them can claim a population of more than 5 lakhs and quite some as few as 10,000 or less, such as Dheyan which has only 6,000 speakers.

The people are popularly called tribals and their languages tribal languages. Majority of these languages belong to the Tibeto-Chinese family and hence have a common heritage and basic foundation. As offshoots of a single ethnic group, the Mongoloid, the people have also some social and behavioural characteristics that, despite their outward differences and dissimilarities, exhibit something common for which they are thought to be one nation, one society, one linguistic circle. But that is not so. In fact they are varied and heterogeneous as others.

Linguistic Unawareness

In the first place, the North-Eastern speech communities are not very much conscious of their linguistic identities. They have rich oral literatures but have not recorded them in writing. As groups of people they remain mostly primitive in their outlook living in antiquated societies. In language culture they did not proceed further.

The Nagas who are apparently one people have an incredibly large number of languages. Eighteen according to 1971 Census, all independent and mutually unintelligible. Why is it so? The answer is that the Nagas, broken into many groups, remained isolated from each other for a long time and, as a result, have failed to develop a linguistic bond between them. The lifestyle and the social set-up of the Nagas are, to some extent, identical everywhere which were not affected due to their isolation from one another. This is because life-styles and social set-ups developed unconsciously in a human society but as for language it is not so. A people must have a definite linguistic idea or else it cannot expect to develop its language. A concrete example of how ignorance affects people's intelligibility is, again, the Nagas. With the 18 or so different languages, the Naga tribes have not been able to maintain intertribe liaison in any one of their languages. They have instead used a broken form of Assamese which serves as the lingua franca of Nagaland even today. Assamese was certainly a foreign language to the Nagas, more foreign and unfamiliar than any one of their own languages. How then did they bring it there? One of the reasons is the dominance and superiority of Assamese over the Naga languages. The ignorance of the tribes about their linguistic affairs is another. In addition, being small tribal speeches, they have never crossed the boundary of their respective villages or circles as their understandability and workability were restricted to those villages and circles only.

Primitive life-style and a philosophical detachment to others, even neighbours and the peculiar topography of the region are also the factors responsible for the tribal societies and languages remaining underdeveloped. The tribal communities are satisfied with their small farmland and ancient mode of agriculture. They never tried to come in contact with the outside world except on a few occasions. This is why their languages remain confined within the walls of, to use Max Muller's words, "the poultry farm" they have beyond which true language begins. They have remained static for nearly two thousand years "as formless, ever moving, anti-horde of dialects" as Grierson puts it. Left to fend for themselves they can easily pass two thousand years more in the same condition without ever developing to anything like a well-developed language. This is, however, not for the fault of north-eastern tribes alone; tribal societies all over the world are responsible for the non-development of their languages.

Bilingualism

More than 75 per cent of the tribal people in north-eastern India are bilingual, their second language being mostly either Assamese or Bengali. Incidentally, the percentage of bilingualism is the highest in this region, 29.76 per cent compared to just 0.18 per cent in Rajasthan which is the lowest. The national average is about 8 per cent. This is due to high ratio of tribal population in north-eastern India.

The diversity of north-eastern tribal mother tongues like those of the Nagas and a high percentage of bilingualism indicate that none of these languages is mature enough to meet the needs of modern age. They were found unsuitable even in earlier times. For this reason both Assamese and Bengali were used as court languages by the states in north-Eastern India for a long time. These states were predominantly tribal, the ruling houses were tribal, the people were tribal. Yet no tribal language was used as court language. Times have changed. Contact with the civilized world has resulted in rapid transformation. From outside are coming in goods and ideas, new, complex and revolutionary. The tribal mother tongues are incapable of expressing all this. Consequently, bilingualism is the solution. Possibility is that percentage of bilingualism among the north-eastern tribal population will considerably increase.

Socio-Politico-Linguistic Confusion

Spread of education as well as political ideas in post-independent era has confused the north-eastern tribal communities. For the first time in their history they begin to think that they are not small groups of people living all alone in their primitive surroundings, segregated from the rest of the world, but are part of a great nation and hence they have a right of their own just like others. So far this is good. The rest is confusion. The recent claim for inclusion of Manipuri and then of Khasi in the Eighth Schedule to Constitution is a case in point. Of the tribal language here, Manipuri is certainly numerically the biggest and literarily most advanced. Khasi which belongs to Austric family is also quite advanced. But they cannot be comparable to much more developed and numerically far more superior languages such as Maithili, Magahi, Bhojpuri, Santali, etc., which are also sufficiently developed with very fine literature and numerical superiority but not incorporated in the Eighth Schedule. And so they have a greater claim. Before their cases are considered, there cannot be any question for Manipuri, Khasi and others (Nepali, a language of another area beyond north-eastern region, has also similar claim) being considered. This is, however, a socio-political and not liguistic move. The cause for it is an obsession with the Eighth Schedule as if inclusion in it meant something big and a status symbol.

The clamour for revival of some ancient scripts is also equally absurd and unfounded. The idea behind this may be due to a misconception widely nursed that language is script and script is language. There is nothing farther from it. In reality the two are completely separate. A language is like a living organism which is too complex to be mastered at minimum effort. A script, on the other hand, is a writing system, much easier, less complex and quite simple. To learn a script one requires hardly a few days' practice but to learn a language a few years tireless effort is not even sufficient. A child picks up a given script during his first few days in school but he learns his mother tongue bit by bit in course of 5 to 10 years. And, interestingly, very few languages of the world have their own scripts. English is the best example. It is written, as are most others in Europe, in a script borrowed from the Romans who borrowed it from the Greeks. The Greeks, again, had borrowed it from the Phoenicians. So if the advanced European languages can have borrowed scripts and continue with them easily and naturally, there is no reason why the less developed tribal languages of north-eastern India cannot go with borrowed scripts. Barring Manipuri and Ahom no other speech communities in this area are known to have any scripts of their own. In fact they have never been reduced to writing before the advent of the Missionaries. Some of them exist only orally still today, with no written literature. In this situation if an ancient script is revived, the languages using it cannot be expected to prosper overnight.

Furthermore, the revival of an old script long in disuse may bring more confusion. It may be found unsuitable after some time. Books written and printed in other scripts will also be rendered useless. And if every community tries to have its own script replacing that in use, there will be a multiplicity of scripts. Such a situation is not ideal for inter-tribe and inter-language communication. A script, moreover, might have practical difficulty. Ahom and Manipuri scripts were discontinued for their limitation. People do not discard a script whose utility has been proven. It is difficult now to discard Roman script for English or German or French languages. On the contrary more and more languages are switching over to it because it is the easiest and most simple. A few years ago S.K. Chatterji advocated the introduction of it for Bengali although Bengali has a well developed script. So if the question of changing a script arises at all, sufficient thought must be given to Roman script and not to others. For the north-eastern speech communities, script is indeed a non-issue.

Fear and Distrust

There is no denying that most of the tribal speeches remain unstudied even till today. We know some of them by their names only and of others not even that, as Grierson wrote more than half a century ago. For the language study native speakers' involvement as well as assistance is very much necessary. There are certain disadvantages for a foreigner/outsider to work on a tribal language. First, his knowledge in these languages is bound to be limited. The work recently done by some outsiders on the tribal languages suffers from many inaccuracies. Most of them for example, have considered Bishnupriya Manipuri as a Tibeto-Burmese language whereas it is nothing but an Indo-Aryan speech closely linked with Bengali and also with Assamese; the speech has only some loans from Meithei. A similar mistake is found in the 1961 Census which omitted Ahom, Khamti and a number of other languages of Siamese-Chinese branch, which are very much living today contrary to popular belief in the outside world. The native speakers may not know the family or families to which their languages belong; they may be ignorant of the special features of their own languages but they certainly know that they have their own languages. If they lend a supporting hand to an outsider scholar working on their language, it is likely that no such mistake or omission occurs.

Inner Strength

The speech communities of north-eastern India have certainly an inner strength of their own. They have lived here long. Yet their speeches remain unaffected, independent and completely separate. But for an inherent strength, it would have never been possible for them to exist independently, especially when the powerful Indo-Aryan languages, Assamese and Bengali are ready in the neighbourhood to grasp them. But that did not happen. Instead, we see a game of interchange between them in which both groups of languages have benefited. This is most clearly visible in case of lexical loans and counter loans. There are innumerable words in many tribal languages which they have borrowed from Bengali and Assamese. Even words of Perso-Arabic origin enter them through Assamese and Bengali. These latter languages in turn have received a fairly large number of words from the former whose history and etymology have been established. There are, again, hundreds of words in Bengali and Assemese whose origin we do not know. A study of the tribal vocabulary may reveal that many of them are in fact from north-eastern tribal languages.

In other areas of language behaviour also similar cross-currents may be traceable. The phenomena like glottal stop in East Bengali dialects or the change of palatal stops to alveolar in both East Bengal dialects and Assamese, etc. remain unexplained. Future linguists may find some clue to them in Tibeto-Burmese languages. But then these languages must first be properly studied. Unfortunately the question of studying them is given little emphasis by scholars simply because they are all underdeveloped languages. Whether they are underdeveloped or not is not a major issue. What concerns us most is that they are understudied, in some cases unstudied also. In this situation it is absurd to determine their importance in scholastic study. The speech communities are again to blame. They have not induced others to take interest in them and their languages. Consequently the outsiders' knowledge about them is faulty and erroneous. It is the duty of the communities themselves, especially those educated and advanced among them, to dispel all misunderstandings. They must also lay the foundation and invite others to do it. Merely asking for a berth in the Constitution will not serve any purpose. They can in good faith demand from the government establishment of a research board or institute specially for the tribal languages. Such a board or institute can do the basic work for development of them. The Universities in this area, too, can take a lead such as the one taken by the North Bengal University for Nepali language.

Tribal societies are well adaptive of new ideas and behaviours. Accordingly what they should do is to come nearer to the advanced neighbouring languages, in particular Assamese and Bengali, and take from them as much as possible. There is no harm if they can take from other rich Tibeto-Chinese languages like Thai, Burmese, etc. In this way they can easily enrich their mother tongues. They need not be afraid of their mother tongues changing their character. Their smallness is their real danger, which they can avert if they combine and become big. Of course in this process the weaker languages may get lost to the stronger ones. That is inevitable and should be viewed as an identification with others. Many weak languages have in the past similarly identified themselves with the stronger ones. If, on the other hand, the tribal communities refuse to accept linguistic loans from and establish contact with the advanced languages and new ideas but turn back toward their primitive ideas, beliefs and linguistic habits, they are sure to get lost for ever. What has happened to the Onges and Jarowas of Andaman and Nicobar Islands? They have refused to come in contact with the civilized world and so are dying out rapidly. Let us hope the north-eastern tribal people will not certainly take a similar course.

REFERENCES

Chatterji, S.K., (1950): 'Kirata-Jana-Kriti', *Journal of Asiatic Society of Bengal,* Letters, Vol. XVI., No. 2, Calcutta.

Dua, Hans R., (1978): *'A Sociolinguistic Profile of India,* LSI Golden Jubilee Volume, Poona.

Grierson, G.A., (1927): *Linguistic Survey of India,* Vol. I, Part I, Calcutta.

Mahapatra, B.P., (1978): *Languages of India—A Brief Survey*, L.S.I. Golden Jubilee Volume, Poona.

Sinha, K.P., (1967): *A Survey on the Bishnupriya Manipuri Language,* Unpub. Ph. D. Diss., Jadavpur University, Calcutta.

Tunga, S.S., (1977): *Bengali and Other Dialects of the District of Cachar: A Comparative and Descriptive Study*, unpub. D.Litt. thesis, Calcutta University, Calcutta.

11

KHASI LANGUAGE AND THE CHANGING SOCIETY

Jeep Sandy Khonglah and
A.P. Sinha

This is a summary of the results of a study conducted to "assess the development in the Khasi language as a consequence of developmental changes experienced by it." The present study begins with three assumptions:

(i) with a change in the society, in its activities and environment, there has to be consequent change in the language which has to develop its own capacity to express the emerging new set of ideas *vis-a-vis* the member of the society (social change-ideas-language sequence);

(ii) the diffusion and adoption of change (cognitive process) in a society to a considerable extent depends on the capacity of the language of the society to precisely communicate them (language-ideas-comprehension); and

(iii) the rate of growth of the vocabulary of a language (repertoire of words as distinct from expression) change comparatively much slower than the rate of growth of its material, social and intellectual aspects.

In the present study in a way it was the second hypothesis which we tried to examine.

The present study was only exploratory, an initial exercise in methodology, and, hence, its results may not be taken so seriously as its technique.

The technique adopted was one of content analysis. It may be enunciated as under :

(i) Listing of all the English verbs in a standard English-Khasi dictionary.

(ii) Writing the Khasi translation of each verb, and putting them into lists, one of those have a single word; Khasi equivalent, and another for those whose Khasi equivalent is a compound (hyphenated) word.

(iii) The English verbs were classified on the basis of Roget's 6 main and 24 subsidiary categories.

(iv) Only four main categories from Roget were used for the purpose of the study. They were:

Main Categories.	*Sub-categories*
Abstract Relations	— relation — change — causation
Intellect	— formation of ideas — communication of ideas
Volition (for action)	— individual action — results of action
Affection (action)	— prospective action — extrinsic action

(v) The nine sub-categories were selected after identifying those directly related to development and the action component for it. A tentative analytical framework was out to test the technique.

The Framework : Modernization refers to action, and action involves the congestion of ideas about the components and processes of action.

There is a need for formation of ideas = Ka *jingpynlong ia ki jingmut* and the communication of ideas = *Pynpaw ia ki jingmut ha kiwei pat.*

— these in turn lead to various forms of relationship = *Ki Jingiadei* between material and non-material thing, and those of cause and effect.

— next is the case of volition, that is the willingness to start action = *Katkum ka mon lane ka Jingjied.*

— if a person (experiencing modernization/change) has to think of new forms of actions he will need to have new words for each.

— to be able to effectively learn new actions there have to be adequate words in the language and then only these actions can be communicated and be within the cognitive capacity of the individual.

The above framework may be something like: a Khasi from the village comes to live in a city. He is expected to have a new set of words to be able to comprehend the new environment and to be able to communicate effectively. For this he will need to have set of words for:

1. formation and communication of ideas;
2. so as to be able to think (cognition) and visualize (comprehension) new forms of relationships;
3. then only will he be able to exercise his willingness (volition) for action; and
4. his action will be based on his judgement of the various forms of causation.

The tentative results have been as follows :

1. **For Action**

(a) *Formation of ideas*: According to the dictionary analysis, it was found that out of the total 232 verbs only 15 verbs did not have single word. These were mostly verbs which referred to formation of ideas for (i) inner satisfaction or (ii) to visualise future action. The Khasi language, however, in respect of this category seemed to be fairly developed now.

(b) *Communication of ideas*: Out of the total 341 verbs in this category, Khasi has single word for 329. This shows that Khasi language is well developed in this respect also. It has however, shown a deficiency in words which refer to communication of ideas through publication, writing and by critical analysis of their meaning (as for example impress, impose, translate, debate, promulgate).

2. **Relation**

This category refers to absolute, continuous or partial relationship. Out of the total 52 verbs for expressing this aspect of ideas,7 do not have any single word. The total list of words in this category according to Rogets is also very small, and hence we can safely say that the Khasi language seems to be developed in this respect also. Between the 7 verbs which do not have any single equivalent in Khasi, complex and circulatory relationships, such as 'correlate', 'dissociate', 'replace' or 'pattern', do not have single equivalents in Khasi. This may be a hindrance in making ideas and communicating finer shades of relationships.

3. **Individual Volition**

There were a total of 73 verbs in this category, out of which 44 had single word Khasi equivalents. In this category the Khasi language does not appear to be well developed as it does not have many analytical words for ideas where imaginary actions are involved.

4. **Causation**

In this category we used 146 verbs, out of which 84 had single word Khasi equivalents. In this category of words which refer to "reproduction", "relation" etc. Khasi has no equivalents. The deficiency can be felt more in the teaching of science subjects and in mechanics and physics. This means that to be able to develop many aspects of scientific thinking, Khasi language will have to progress and coin new words.

5 and 6. **Affection**

We noted 102 verbs in this category out of which 62 have single word Khasi equivalents. For both prospective and extrinsic affection, Khasi has suitable words for common action. But such actions of pride, such as 'boast', 'bolster', 'reassure' do not have appropriate words.

7. **Result of Action**

There were 36 verbs in this category and 19 had single word equivalents. Khasi appears to be well developed in the ideas of this category.

8. **Change**

Khasi has in all 71 verbs in this category which refer to actions of change, out of which 36 have been expressed by compound words. This is not a sign of development of the language.

As an overall assessment, it can be said that the Khasi language has shown encouraging signs of development. Further studies need, however, to be made for more reliable evaluation so as to be able to assess whether the Khasi language is able to cope with various forms of ideas associated with development and allied cognitive phenomena, i.e. the proficiency factor.

Out of the total 1030 verbs listed, 517 had single word equivalents.

12

SINO-TIBETAN LANGUAGES OF NORTH-EAST INDIA
Social Aspects

Pramod Chandra Bhattacherji

The North-Eastern India comprising of the present-day Assam, Meghalaya, Arunachal, Nagaland, Mizoram, Manipur and Tripura and quite distantly, some parts of West Bengal (Coochbehar, Jalpaiguri districts) and adjoining areas of Bangladesh presents a mixed and varied population of diverse ethnic groups and linguistic families with some elements of social as well as cultural affinities since the ages of *Ramayana* and the *Mahabharata* when this north-eastern territories of *Bharatvarsa* was known as *Pragjyotish, Lauhitya, Kamarupa-Kamakhya* and the like inhabited mostly by the Kiratas or so-called Mongoloids (*Siddeshi Yoginipithe dharmah Kairataia matah*).

Grierson, Chatterji, Robert Shafer and others have dealt with the Sino-Tibetan languages as well as the speakers in their writings from different points of view. Since 1951, the writer has also been dealing with a Sino-Tibetan speech of North-Eastern India, namely Boro or Boro-Kachari (Plains Kachari) which differ from Dimasa or Hills Kachari of the North-Cachar district areas in some linguistic features and resembles Garo of Meghalaya in a number of linguistic peculiarities. Apart from the speakers of the Sino-Tibetan family of languages the population of Assam also comprises speakers of the Indo-European (Indo-Aryan) family, the Austric (Kahsi-Synteng), and the Dravidian (Tamil, Telugu etc.) families of languages.

Without going into the classification of Sino-Tibetan or Tibetan-Chinese family of languages after Grierson or Robert Shafer (which is dealt in the writer's work: *A Descriptive Analysis of the Boro Language,* 1977), the writer would like to quote a few lines from S.K. Chatterji from his *'Kirata-Jana-Kriti'* (1951) "The area of characterisation for the primitive Sino-Tibetan speech appears to have been North-Western China between the headwaters of the Huang Ho and the Yangtsze Kiang rivers... Mongoloid tribes from Western China speaking forms of the Sino-Tibetan speech appear to have been pushing south and west from their original homeland from pre-historic times, but certain large-scale movements of which we have faint inklings seem to have begun in the early part of the first millennium B.C. ... the Bodos, who spread over the whole of the Brahmaputra valley and North Bengal as well as East Bengal, forming a solid block in North-Eastern India, were the most important Indo-Mongoloid people in Eastern India, and they form one of the main bases, of the present-day population of these tracts..." B. Kakati in his *Assamese, Its Formation and Development* (1941) deals with the structure and phonology of Assamese language and the probable Sino-Tibetan (Boro) elements in Assamese. J.D. Anderson pointed out to the syntax of Assamese and Bengali correlated to the Sino-Tibetan Boro parallels.

The Sino-Tibetan languages family in India is the smallest from the point of population strength, but largest in the number of languages being as many as 51 in 1971 Census. According to an analysis given by B.P. Mahapatra (1978) on the basis of 1971 Census of India, this language family is broadly divided into two main branches, Siamese-Chinese and Tibeto-Burmans. The number of speakers of the Tibeto-Burmese is 4,329,405 roughly 0.79 per cent of our population. The Tibeto-Burmese branch is divided into three main sub-branches : Tibeto-Himalaya, North-Assam and Assam-Burmese. The languages of the Bhotia group under the Tibeto-Himalayan sub-branches includes Sikkimese Bhotia as well as Monpa of Arunachal. The North-Assam sub-branch is represented by Adi (Abor), Nissi (Dafla), Mishmi in Arunachal and Mishing (Miri) in Assam. The Assam-Burman sub-branch with its five groups represents 30 languages of the Sino-Tibetan stock. Kachin groups is not represented by any language in India, while Burmese is represented by Mogh spoken in Tripura numbering 12,378. The Boro (Bodo) group consists of nine languages, such as Boro (Boro-Kachari), Lalung (Tiwa), Dimasa (Hill Kachari), Rabha (Raidongias only), Deori (Chutiya), Mikir (Karbi) of Assam state, Garo and Koch from Meghalaya (Garo Hills district) and Tripuri (Trpra) from Tripura. The Naga group of languages consists of 18 (eighteen) languages such as Angami, Sema, Khezha, Ao, Lotha, Ghang, Konyak, Zeliang, Sangtam, Phom, Yimchungre, Khiemnungam all from Nagaland ; Kabui, Mao, Tangkhul from Manipur; Nocte, Wancho and Tangsa from Arunachal. The Kuki-Chin group consists of Meithei (Manipuri), Thado, Paite, Hmar, Vaiphei, Kuki of Manipur, Lakher, Lushai (Mizo), Pawri of Mizoram (Lushai Hills district) and Halam from Tripura. This short survey is not complete and far from accurate. There is an urgent need of a fresh survey from descriptive linguistic point of view.

The study of Sino-Tibetan languages of North-Eastern India is at an incipient stage. The linguistic work done by the Naga Institute of Culture from Kohima, the Arunachal Pradesh administration, the Manipur administration, the Central Institute of Indian languages, Mysore, the Government of Assam as well Meghalaya through the auspices of Tribal Research Institutes and the research projects undertaken by the Universities of Gauhati and Dibrugarh demands a systematic collaboration as well as a comprehensive attempt either through some agencies in the North-Eastern Hill University and the North Eastern Council at an early date to ascertain the proper perspective of the problems of Sino-Tibetan language as well as the speakers from the point of mother-tongue, medium of teaching, bilingualism as well as the socio-linguistic aspects of the people of North-Eastern India.

The scheduled languages of the Indian Union such as Assamese, Bengali and Hindi are used and spoken by the people of North-Eastern India including the considerable speakers of the Sino-Tibetan family of languages. The use of English as a second language in Meghalaya, Mizoram, Nagaland and some areas of North-Eastern India is a topic of deeper analysis and the substitute of Hindi as a national language in place of English, the alternative link national language of India should be viewed and reviewed in the changing background of North-Eastern India with sentiments of the speakers who are more or less associated with the primitive or Kirata forms of religion, matriarchal as well as mixed patriarchal family structures as well as socio-cultural ceremonies of birth, marriage and death. The languages and dialects play an important role in respect of village community within a regional society and the social aspects of the languages and dialects including mother tongues are vital to the tribal people.

Within a limited sphere as well as with frank confession to his own limitations, the writer may be permitted to opine that the Sino-Tibetan languages as well as dialects of North-Eastern India in an atmosphere of predominantly Indo-European as well as Indo-Aryan influences of loan-words and super-cultural items, need further scientific and systematic analysis and study at all levels.

13

A SHORT NOTE ON MISING PHONOLOGY*

Tabu Taid

The Language

MISING is a Tibeto-Burman language spoken by about half a million Misings (or Miris as they have been generally known hitherto) residing in the districts of Lakhimpur, Dibrugarh, Sibsagar and Darrang in the state of Assam as well as in some areas of the Siang district of Arunachal. Its closest cognates are the speeches of the Adis in the Siang and Lohit districts of Arunachal, particularly the speeches of the Pasis, the Padams, the Pangis, the Milangs and the Minyongs. The speeches of some other communities of Arunachal, viz. the Hrussos (or the Akas), the Nisis (or the Daflas), the Gallongs and the Mishmis form distant cognates of Mising. Owing to the absence of written records, it is extremely difficult to reconstruct the prototype of these speeches, and, to the best of my knowledge, no attempt has been made so far to do anything of the kind. It may not, however, be all that difficult to reconstruct an Adi-Mising prototype, but, again, no comparative studies of these speech forms have been done which would have made such a reconstruction possible.

Mising has a few varieties within it, viz., Oyan, Dambug, Delu,

*This paper represents, more or less, the summary of a dissertation submitted by the author to the Department of Linguistic Science, University of Reading, U.K. in 1974.

Moying, Pagro, Sayang and Somuang these names representing the various social groups within the Mising community. The varieties show some phonological, morphological and lexical divergences, but hardly and syntactic variation. No Mising ever has much difficulty in understanding any of these varieties.

Although Mising folklore is fairly rich, the language is yet to have a stable written tradition. Sporadic attempts have been made over the years to publish books and journals, but there has never been any vigorous literary effort on the part of the Misings. A section of educated Mising youths have, in recent years, been making attempts at evolving a scientific writing system for the language as a prelude to the expected growth of a written tradition in the near future.

The Phonemes

Mising has a phonemic system of fifteen consonants and fourteen vowels. Of the fifteen consonants, six, all unaspirated, are stops and nine continuants including four nasals, two fricatives, one lateral, one trill and one frictionless continuant. The fourteen vowels may neatly be divided into two halves—seven long and seven short. Each of the seven short vowels has its long counterpart. Of these seven, two are front, two back and three central.

Apart from these phonemes, a few more sounds, viz: (w), (tc), (dz) and (h) are heard in the language. But none of these sounds has phonemic value in the language.

The phonemes are given below in tabular forms. Phonemes /p, t, k, s/ are voiceless, the rest being voiced.

The Consonants

	Bilabial	Dental	Alveolar	Palatal	Velar
Stop	p b	t d			k g
Nasal	m		n	p	y
Lateral			l		
Trill			r		
Fricatives			s z		
Frictionless Continuant				j	

The Vowels

	Front	Central	Back
High	i :, i	ɨ :, ɨ	u :, u
Mid	e :, e	ə :, ə	o :, o
Low		a :, a	

The Stops

The stops are produced by light contacts between articulator and point of articulation. Thus for /p,b/, there is a soft bilabial contact for /t.d/ a soft apico-dental contact and for /-k.g/ a soft dersovelar contact. In other words, the 'plosion' in the case of the Mising plosives is very mild (and so they are not quite like the English plosives in the manner of their articulation).

All the stops occur freely in word-initial and word-medial positions. Examples:

/po : pɨr/	'butterfly'
/tattɨg/	'toad', 'frog'
/ko : kan/	'children'
/babɨn/	'a kind of aram'
/do : de:/	'peacock'
/gun : gan/	'harp made of bamboo', etc.

In word-final positions, the vioced-voiceless contrast is neutralised. It is not easy to decide whether word-final stops is Mising are the voiceless /p.t.k/ or the fully devoiced forms of /b,d.g/. On strictly phonetic grounds we should say that only /p,t,k/ and not /b,d,g/ occur finally in Mising. But, when morph-ononemic considerations are brought in, it is possible to think of word-final /p,t,k/ as fully devoiced forms of /b,d,g/. Let us see what happens to the following words when the Third Person nominative suffix /ə/ is added to them :

/talap/	('onion', 'garlic')	+	{—ə}	—	/talabə/
/tabat/	('sugarcane')	+	{—ə}	—	/tabadə/
/porok/	('hen')	+	{—ə}	—	/porogə/

This is like German /bund /which is phonetically bunt, but which becomes (bund) when it is followed by the morpheme [—es]; (bunt) + [es] — [bundes]. If, however, we leave aside morpho- phonology at this point, it can be safely concluded on phonetic principles that / b,d,g/ do not occur in word-final positions.

The Nasals

There are four nasals, viz. / m, n, / in the language, of which /m,n,n/ occur in all the three positions. The lamino-alveolar nasal / / occurs only in initial and medial positions. In one of the dialects of Mising, / / occurs only in medial positions. Although it is unmistakably a phoneme in the language, its occurrence is not very frequent.

Examples :

Initially and medially :

/ma : mo/	'elder sister-in law'
/na : noi/	'father's younger brother's wife'
/yə goy/	'crawling about'
/ya : yi/	'mother-in-law', 'father's sister' or mother's brother's wife

Word-finally :

/rokom/	'Early in the morning'
/rokon/	'the other morning'
/rokoy/	'to move across stealthily'

The Lateral and the Trills

The voiced alveolar lateral /1/ is of the clear kind and occurs in all three positions, though its occurrence in the final position is rather infrequent. The trill /r/ is slightly unstable in quality and has a number of idiolectic variations ranging from the rolled to the frictionless continuant. It also occurs in all the three positions.

Examples :

Initially and Medially :

/lolat/	'moonlight'
/ru : rual/	'din'

Finally :

/amal/	'(jocular for) money'
/do : mtr/	'sky'

The Fricatives

There are just two fricatives in the language, *viz.*, /s/ and /z/, the friction, as in the case of 'plosion' of the stops, being mild. Both the sounds occur in initial and medial positions. /s/ occurs finally in certain onomatopoetic words and loan-words but /z/ does not occur finally. Finally /a/ in loan-words are transformed into /s/.

Example :

Initially and Medially :

/si : say/	'adolescent'
/zo : zibtlty/	'lizard'

Finally :

/bakos/	'box'
/koros/	'expenditure'

The Frictionless Continuant

The voiced lamino-palatal semivowel /j/ occurs in all the three positions, e.g. /ja : jo/ 'grandmother', /kaj/ 'come'. Final /j/ may also be described as forming a diphthong with a preceding vowel.

Additional Consonant Sounds

It has already been mentioned that /w/, /tc/ and /dz/ occur as phones in the language, though not as phonemes. When there is a transition from /u/ to /a,o, i,ə/, the resultant phoneme is the semivowel /w/. Again, when a morpheme ends with either /o:/ or /u:/ and is linked with a suffix beginning with a vowel, the linking is done by the insertion of /w/ which replaces the vowel length. Example:

/biu/	(festival) + /ə/ (nominativiser)	=	[biw ə]
/tou/	(cooking pot) + /*t*:/ (intensifier)	=	[tow*t*:]
/ko:/	(boy) + /ə/ (nominativiser)	=	[kow ə]
/su:/	(at present) + /o:/ (intensifier)	=	[suwo:] etc.

The gemination of the two alveolar fricatives /s/ and /z/ sometimes results in the production of tc and dz. Again, when /s/ and /pz/ are preceded respectively by /t/ and /d/, /s/ and /z/ become affricates /tc/ and /dz/, for example

/matsik/	=	mattcik	'small sword'
/adzi :/	=	addzi :	'small'

/asi/ (water) + /ə/ (nominativiser) = /assə/ = [attcə]
/pəzi/ (kind of poisonous leaf) + /ə/ = /pəzz/ = pəddzə.

The glottal fricative /h/ occurs in one of the dialects as an allophone of /s/ in intervocalic positions, e.g. /gasor/ 'sheet of cloth worn over the body' = [gahor]. It does not occur in any other environment. Thus, it is quite clear that [w], [tc], [dz], and [h], which are of resultant character, cannot be accorded phonemic status in the language.

Consonant Clusters and Gemination

Clusters of only two consonants occur in Mising and they occur only in word-medial positions. Clusters do not form part of a syllable. The two members of a cluster belong to two different syllables, e.g. /jab-go/ 'door'; /ap-ta/ 'hunting'; /lam - tə/ 'road' etc.

Gemination in Mising may be defined simply as a consonant cluster consisting of two identical consonants on both sides of a syllable boundary, e.g. /ap-pi:/ 'four'; /zab-bo/ 'gander' etc.

There are ninety-one consonants clusters in the language. In one of the dialects, viz. Sa :yang, the number of consonants clusters is one hundred and three; the twelve clusters which occur in this dialect and not in the others are the clusters of /1/ followed by /t,d,k,g,m,n,*p,p,*s,z,r,j,/.* The ninety-one clusters (including geminates) are:

/p/, /t/, /k/followed by, /*p*,t,k,s/	=	12
/b/ followed by /b,d,g,n,m,l,z,r,j/	=	11
/d/ followed by /b,d,g,z/	=	4
/g/ followed by /b,d,g,m,n,*p,p*,l,z,r,j/	=	10
/m/ followed by /p,t,k,b,a,g,m,n,*p,p,* l/s,z,r,j./	=	15
/n/ followed by /p,t,k,b,d,g,m,n,*p,p,*l,s,z,r,j/	=	15
/ / followed by /k,g,m,n,n/	=	5
/l/ followed by /p,b,l/	=	3
/r/ followed by /p,t,k,b,d,g,m,n,*p,p*,l,s,z,r,j/	=	15
/j/ followed by /j/	=	1

It may be noted that no clusters 'can be formed with / , s, z,/ as first member. There may be a few more clusters with /j/ as first member, if the diphthongs /ai, oi, ui, əi/are treated as /aj, oj, uj, əj/

Vowels and Diphthongs

Mising has a well-balanced vowel system of four-front, four back and six central articulations. The spreading and rounding of lips are not very prominent.

The Front Vowels

/i:/ and /i/ are the long and short high unrounded vowels slightly lower than cardinal /i/. The quantitative difference affects their quality. Thus /i:/ is slightly higher than /i/. They occur in all three positions /e:/ and /e/ are the long and short mid-unrounded vowels

* Most of these clusters, however, occur in loan-words used in the various dialects.

lower than cardinal /e/. There is hardly any qualitative difference between the two. They occur in all three positions.

The Back Vowels

/O:/ and /o/ are the long and short rounded vowels in the half-open position, much lower than cardinal /o/. There is hardly any qualitative difference between the two /U:/ and /u/ are the long and short rounded vowels approximating the position of cardinal /u/. The long /u:/ is higher than the short /u/. The four back vowels occur in all the three positions.

The Central Vowels

/a:/ and /a/ are the long and short unrounded low vowels. The long /a:/ is lower and 'backer' than the short /a/.

/ə:/ and /ə/ are the mid-unrounded long and short central vowels. There is hardly any qualitative difference between the two. /t:/ and /t/ are the long and short high central vowels. /t:/ is higher than /t/. All the six central vowels occur in all the three positions.

Contrasts illustrated

/i/	/kinam/	'to be sick'
/i:/	/ki:nam/	'to pull'
/e/	/kenam/	'to take a bite'
/e:/	/ke:nam/	'to hook'
/o/	/konam/	'to ask (for something)'
/o:/	/ko:nam/	'to ferry across'
/u/	/kunam/	'to shout'
/u:/	/ku: nam/	'to be sour'
/a/	/kanam/	'to have'
/a:/	/ka:nam/	'to see'
/ə/	/kənam/	'to take (someone's) side'
/ə:/	/kə:nam/	'to prepare (curry)'
/t/	/ptnam	'to pour'
/t:/	/pt:nam/	'to reach', 'to suffice'

Vowel Length in the Word-final Positions

Like the loose of voiced-voiceless opposition of stops in the word final position, vowels, too, lose the short long contrast in this position. There is probably just one minimal pair in the language showing the short-long phonemic contrast word-finally.

/ake/ 'some'
/ake:/ 'a bunch (of, say, thread)'

However, the native speaker realises the short long opposition in both production and perception, and the addition of suffixes makes the opposition obvious. Thus, the long vowel in /ko:/ 'boy' may not be prominent when the word is uttered in its bare form, but it stands out clearly when we add the definite article suffix {-də}:-/ko:/ + {də} = [ko: də] 'the boy'.

But the freedom of occurrence with length in the final position is not shared equally by all the vowels. The front vowels /i:/ and /e:/ occur in a large number of words; /o:/, /e:/ and /t:/ occur chiefly in monosyllabic words which are far from numerous; /a:/ and /u:/ occur in rare cases.

Diphthongs

The vowel system in Mising includes eighteen diphthongs, *viz.*

(i) Diphthongs ending in /i/ = /ai, oi, ui, əi/
(ii) „ „ „ /a/ = /ea, oa, ua, əa, ta/
(iii) „ „ „ /o/ = /ao, to/
(iv) „ „ „ /u/ = /iu, au, ou, əu, əu/
(v) „ „ „ /i/ = /at, et/

Some of these diphthongs, *viz.*, /ea, oa, əa, ta, oa, to/ may be bisected to form two different syllables.

Three-vowel clusters

If we leave aside the cases of glides from /u/, as the second member of a three-vowel cluster, to /a, o, t, ə/ which results in the production of the semi-vowel /w/, there will be just one instance of triphthongisation, viz. /a, tə/.

Syllabic Structure

The syllable in a Mising word may be represented as (c) v (c). There are no initial or final consonant clusters, as has already been noted. The syllable types are:

(i)	V	-	/i:/	'blood'	/ə:/	'yes'
(ii)	CV	-	/no/	'you'	/ro:/	'morning'
(iii)	VC	-	/a:m/	'paddy'	/t:r/	'gorgeous'
(iv)	CVC	-	/ga:m/	'chieftain'	/nom/	'you' (accusative)

Structure of Disyllabic Words

The vast majority of the underived forms of words in the language is disyllabic. The two syllables in those words may combine in the following ways:

V + V	/ta/	'bamboo'
V + CV	/oy/o	'fish'
CV + V	/pao/	'A mising surname'
CV + CV	/do: pi/	'the sun'
CV + VC	/loum/	'three days'
CV +CVC	/kopak/	'banana'
VC + CV	/appi:/	'four'
VC + CVC	/argom/	'rust'
CVC + CV	/kampu/	'white'
CVC + CVC	/sormon/	'crocodile'
V + VC	/at n/	'gold'
V + CVC	/agom/	'language'

Supra-segmented Features

Word-stress is weak in Mising. In the case of words with two or more syllables, the stress is realised consistently in the second syllable. Sentence-stress, however, is prominent. Examples :

/a'ppi:/ - /a'ppi:ko/ - /a'ppi:kolang/ -
/a'ppi:kom*t*lo:m n/ etc.

Mising is not a tone language.

Two degrees of intonation can be heard, viz. rise and fall. But, the realisation of these differs from dialect to dialect, sometimes from village to village.

Conclusion

As a pioneering study of Mising phonology, the treatment above may require minor modifications here and there, particularly with reference to the dialects in the language. It can, however, be legitimately hoped that it will duly serve as a dependable stepping stone for fuller and more sophisticated treatments on the subject.

14

A FEW ASPECTS OF SOME OF THE LANGUAGES OF ARUNACHAL PRADESH

K. Das Gupta

Arunachal Pradesh which is inhabited by twenty-five tribes has a population of about 4, 41,744. Some of these tribes are divided into sub-tribes or groups and each group has its own dialect. The distribution of tribes in different districts are as follows:

Kameng	:	Monpa, Sherdukpen, Khoa, Aka, Nishi, Sulung and Bangru.
Subansiri	:	Tagin, Nishi, Hill Miri, Apatani, Sulung and Bangrus.
Siang	:	Adis, Memba and Khambas.
Lohit	:	Mishmi, Khamti, Singpho and Adis.
Tirap	:	Nocte, Wancho, Tangsa and Singpho.

The Adi is a general name for a number of tribes such as: Gallong, Minyong, Padam, Pasi, Bori, Bokar, Pailibo, Ramo and Milang.

The three tribes Idu, Digaru and Miji are known as Mishmis. The Tangsas of the Tirap District are divided into twelve groups, namely, Longchang, Moklum, Kimsing, Jogli, Mosang. Tikhak, Rongrang, Hawi (Havi), Morang, Longri, Panthei and Tutsa.

There are a few pockets where the differences in dialects with the neighbouring areas are so marked that they may be treated as "linguistic islands" and such islands are found in Tirap, Soha Nocte, and in Kameng, Lish Monpa.

Though there are twenty-five tribes speaking about sixty to seventy dialects the question of distinguishing language from dialects does not arise at this stage. None of the tribes has a script except Khamti which has one,— a variety of the Shan script of Burma. The Monpa uses Tibetan script for religious scriptures. A few years back Assamese was the medium of instruction in the school stage which has now been replaced by English. Some of the major dialects were experimented with as mediums of instruction for primary education and texts books in devanagari script were produced, but the schemes had to be abandoned for various reasons. English has been introduced as a medium of instruction in the primary and secondary stage of school from 1974. At present English as well as Hindi is the medium of instruction.

For a linguist, there is no difference between a language and a dialect. Each dialect can express anything needed for the society and so it is as good as any other dialect. But this difference is marked when we study it from socio-linguistic view points. One of the dialects gains some importance owing to some reason and then it becomes a language and is accepted as a norm for other dialect groups. The Philological Section of the Research Department of Arunachal Pradesh has given scripts to the major languages and has codified the lexicons. A number of books dealing with different aspects of the languages have been published. Articles also have been published to bring the language to the common field of knowledge.

The languages of Arunachal Pradesh are rich in vocabulary and expression pertaining to their culture and the native people can express their mind in a very concise manner giving every detail of activities necessary for their social life. Geographical features, social life and ecology have some important role in shaping the mental attitude of the people which is reflected in the verbal expression. So when we study these languages we may be familiar with their concepts and their way of looking at things. In Singpho, a language of Tirap District there is no separate word for the relational terms "mother", "father" and "brother". The pronominal element is inseparable from the word. It is expressed as: *any*—my mother, *imu*—your mother, *gnu*—his mother. When I asked the informant

"How is it that there is no separate word for "father", "mother" etc. in your language?" He retorted "How could it be, mother has to be somebody's mother". This is, however, in conformity with the Hegelian notion that "every idea is a group of relation, and we can think of something only by relating to something else".

For the expression " I have lost my way", the Nishi use *"ngo lampya ka-pa-ku-ma"* meaning thereby "I am not finding the way". They will not use the word "lose" in this context. They argue that the road is already there and that it is not a money bag which one can lose. There is nothing illogical in that way of thinking and we cannot but appreciate the logic behind it.

In counting objects, the number is not directly linked to the objects qualified but through some classificatory particles. These classifiers indicate certain classes into which all objects are grouped—shape, size, etc.

In Nishi : *Kar* for ear ornament worn by men, *bum* for long object, *aking*—one, *anyi*—two, *gagi kar-king*—one ear ornament, *ehe' bum-nyi*—two bamboos.

"Every number is a plurality of thought held together and to that extent it is a unity". So there is nothing unusual that they classify different classes of things.

Genetically, the languages belong to Tibeto-Burman family except Khamti which belongs to the Thai group. Structurally, the languages are agglutinative though the degree of glutination may vary and it is well marked in Adi, Nishi, Apatani and Hill Miri. In an agglutinative language some particles which have no independent existence express meaning when hooked together like a chain in a sentence.

So to learn the language one has to master the use of these particles : *gi-go, dung*-continuative suffix.

In Minyong :	*ngo gi-dong*	:	I go, I am going.
	ngo gi-li-dung	:	I wish to go.
	ngo gi-go-li-dung	:	I wish to move (aimlessly).
	ngo gi-man-li-dung	:	I wish to move about for enjoyment.
	ngo gi-po-li-dung	:	I wish to move before starting any work.

In the above example, *li*—for wish, *go*—for here and there and *man*—for enjoyment are inserted to differentiate shades of meaning. Similarly, in Gallong :

mennam	:	to speak
men-pak-nam	:	to make a clear-cut speech
men-kap-nam	:	to explain
men-tup-nam	:	to make a faltering speech
men-bo-nam	:	to suppress one in discussion, i.e. to impose one's authority over another
men-sir-nam	:	to advise
men-si-nam	:	to whisper

As activities like discussion, advising, whispering etc., involve speaking all such meanings are derived from *men-nam* to speak.

A language is the mirror of a culture. So culture of the people is exhibited in verbal expression. Tribal people move about in different villages for various purposes and they take meals at the homes of their friends. The word *nibo* meaning guest for "outsider" is to be distinguished from *aging* which indicates reciprocity of guesthood.

In Bori :	*do*		*eat*
	su	:	reflexive
	ngo do-ing-ting	:	I am taking meal at my home
	ngo do-su-dung	:	I am taking my own meal or at my house

In Moklum Tangsa, both *jatom* and *lingtom* are used to mean "thrice". But *jatom* is used if one takes meal in one's own house and *lingtom* is used if one goes outside and takes one's meal at another's house. To most other languages such distinction does not exist.

A language is always responsive to its situation, the topography and natural surroundings. Relative distance, visibility and invisibility of a person in relation to the speaker have a significant role in these languages. The pronouns have different forms to denote, same level, higher and lower level and up and down the hill.

In Nishi : *asam*	:	Him (nearby, same level)
alam	:	Him (at a little distance)
te'-lam	:	Him (up the hill)
be'-lam	:	Him (down the hill)

Two demonstrative pronouns, *ira* and *iri,* equivalent to the English "this" occur in Moklum Tangsa. *Ira* indicates something that is particularised for imminent action and *iri* denotes an unspecified object, action in respect of which, may occur in future.

ira i kitap	:	This is my book
iri utang kitap	:	Whose book is this?

Aspects (kinds of action) rather than the time as indicated by the tense in English are main features of the language.

In Minyong : *do*	:	eat
ngo do-to	:	I ate
ngo do-to-bong	:	I finished my meal (irrespective of what was in my plate)
ngo do-yin-to	:	I ate up (everything)
ngo do-bong-to	:	I ate excessively.

In Miju, verbs denoting performance followed by departure have different forms.

gram rong-shu	:	Pack the load
roi-tha	:	Go after packing
dam-shu	:	Beat (imp)
dai-tha	:	Go after beating

Vowel harmony is a characteristic feature of the Miju. The negative prefix *ma, mo* and *mi* conform with the degree of openness of the vowel of the verb.

mi-ship-yung	:	(I) do not buy
ma-tat-yung	..	I do not understand

In Nocte the negative indicates both the subject and object relation and assumes a conjugation pattern. *Ko*—give, *nga*—I

nga-ma ate-uang ko-mak	: I will not give him
nga-ma nang-nang ko-mi	: I will not give you
ni-ma ne-nang ko-ma	: We will not give you (pl)

Distinctive tones occurs in almost all the languages of Arunachal Pradesh though it has been found only in a few cases in Adi languages. Words have different meanings with different tones though the spelling is the same. In Singpho *nga* (abrupt rising)—Fish *nga* (level)—Be. live, *nga* (rising)—Buffalo.

In Singpho as well as in some other languages adjectives are generally verbs attributing quality to the form : *ong*—glad, *ngai ong-ha-dai*—I was glad.

Natural beauty is also distinguished from artificial beauty.

Shra ndai-wa sop-de	: The place is beautiful
tebul-wa com-de	: The table is beautiful

The Monpa verb is impersonal. They are concerned more with the state of happening than with the time of occurrence. So there is no clearly defined tense system in Monpa and the present, past and future often cut across each other and the indication of time is sepecified more precisely by the aspects denoted by some particles. The use of particles is dependant on the final sound of the root.

U occurs with roots that elide final *K*
gok —roast; *sha go-u*—roast mea
thak—boil; *tochang tha-u*—boil rice

Khu is taken by root ending in valar nazal
thing—stand; *thing-khu* —stand up
dong—cut; *ma-dong-khu*— Do not cut

Three characteristic features are noticed in the behaviour of the verbs in languages of Arunachal Pradesh.

The verbs in the Adi group of languages do not indicate person and number and the same suffix is used for different persons and numbers. The verb in Nocte and Tangsa indicate different persons and numbers *(nga hum-nang ka-tak*—I went home; *ni hum-nang-ka-ti*—We went home; *ate ka-ta*—He went) where as in Monpa, the suffix is dependent on the final sound of the verb; voiced or unvoiced etc.

The languages belong to the Tibeto-Burman group and some kind of correspondence among the different languages are noticed. Benedict gives a classification: Adi, Miri, Nishi and Nocte and other Naga groups have a cleavage through an intermediate Kachin (Singpho) stage which is exhibited in the relationship given below. This relation holds good in respect of some languages of Arunachal Pradesh.

The initial component of a consonant cluster of the Singpho has been retained in Gallong.

	Singpho	Gallong
House	*nta*	*nam*
Hot	*kthet*	*agu*
Abuse	*blep*	*bu*
Arrow	*pla*	*upuk*

In some cases the initial consonant in Singpho has been dropped in Gallong.

	Singpho	Gallong
Flower	*aban*	*apu*
Call	*sga*	*gok*
Buy	*mri*	*re*

The voiced velar stop in Singpho corresponds to non-voiced stop in Miju (g-K)

	Singpho	Miju
Sharp	*grang*	*krat*
Quickly	*glau*	*klau*
Shoot	*gap*	*kep*

Again Notce has retained the initial consonant of the Miju.

	Miju	Nocte
Cold	*krong*	*aki*
Soup	*tlam*	*ti*
Fasten	*kro*	*akhak*

It has also been dropped.

	Miju	Nocte
Road	*blong*	*lam*
Tongue	*blai*	*the-li*

In *spite* of the differences among various languages in Arunachal Pradesh, we find likenesses in words, in the use of classifiers and in the economy of thought which is exhibited by different aspects.

(The sound of 'O' is as open as in the English 'not', 'c' is palatal. The vowel 'e' is centralized in some words.)

REFERENCES

Das Gupta, K., An Introduction to Central Monpa; An Introduction to the Nocte Language; An Introduction to the Gallong Language; Pattern of Inter-relationship among the Languages of Arunachal; *RESARUN*, vol. 3. No. 2, April 1977.

Grierson, G.A., *Linguistic Survey of India,* Vol. III.

Paul K, Benedict, *Sino-Tibetan A Conspectus,* Contributing, Editor Matsoff, J. A.

INDEX

Acculturation, 107
Adi-Missing, 134
Adivasi, 80
Administrative units, linguistic
  redistribution of, 59
Adult education programmes, 86
Advid Bharat, 28
Aghast, 101
Agitation, 55
Ahoms, 102-03
Ahom-Manipuri scripts, 120-21
Allen, B.C., 62
Allen, W.J., 42, 71-72
American Baptist Mission, 50
Amlahs, 36
Anderson, J.D., 131
Anglo-Khasi war, 34, 38
Anglo-vernacular Text-Book
  Committee, 53
Apatani language, 12
Arabic terms, 111
Arrogance, 12
Articulation, 136, 140
Arunachal Pradesh,
  classification particles, 147
  conjugation patterns, 150
  demonstrative pronouns, 149
  distinctive tones, 150
  languages, 145-50
    relation terms, 146
  scene, 74-75
  vowel harmony, 149-50
Arunoday, 50
Ascending generation, kinship
  terms in, 97-98
Assam administration, 49
Assam Association, formation of,
  61
Assam Congress Government, 64
Assam, further progress, 53-54
  multilingual composition,
    66
  police reaction, 55-56
Assamese, Bengali script, 78, 80
  borrowed words, 114-15
  culture, 104-05
  demand for restoration, 50
  language, 57-58, 84
  loan words, 115-16
  nationality-formation, 23-24
  voice heard, 50-51
Assamese Text Book hurdle,
  52-53
Assessment, 14
Assimilation, 14, 21, 24
Awareness, celebration of, 14
Axioms, 89

Bandyopadhyay, P.K., 69
Bangladesh, 130

Banyans, 32
Baptist Missionaries, 32, 35, 38, 69
Bardoloi Government, 65
Barooah, Nirode K., 36
Baruah, Jaduram, 58
Bayley, Stuart, 53
Bengal administration, 49
Bengalees, 50-51, 52, 54-57
    committees, 113
    expansionism, 24
    immigrants, 62
    language, 12, 26, 28, 58-60
        status of, 27
    population, 57, 61-62
Bhagyachandra, Rajarishi, 77
Bhakatiya Bhaha, 106
Bhattacharji, Pramod Chandra, 130
Bhattacharji, Jayanta Bhusan, 26
Bhattacharya, Shyamdas, 26
Bhojpuri language, 120
Bhutanese language, 36
Bilingualism, 119-20, 132
Bodo language, 90
Boro (Bodo) group, language, 132
Boro-Kachari tribal population, 25
Borrowed words, 114-15
Brahmaputra valley, 49-50, 56, 60, 64, 77
Brahmo movement, 45
Brahmo Samaj, 43-44
British administration, 40
British policy-pragmatism, 49-50
British Raj, 26, 31
Buddhist chakma tribe, 26
Buranjis chronicles, 111
Burma dominions, 33

Calcutta University, 44, 58, 64
Campbell, A.E., 51
Carey, William, 32-33, 36
Chakravarty, Nilmoni, 44
Chatterji, S.K., 121, 131
Chawai (Datta), 99
Cherrapunji, 34, 38
Chinese language, 89
Choudhury, Rohini Kumar, 65
Christian missionaries, 69-70
Col. Hughton, 51
Colonial administration, 36
Colonialism, stress and strain of, 30-32
Commerce and industry, new system words, 113
Commercialisation, 106
Commissioner of Assam valley, 53, 55, 56-57
Communications, 105, 107-08
    indigenous system, 84-85
    of ideas, 127
Communist China-trained revolutionaries, 81
Conflicting attitude, 63-64
Conjugation pattern, 150
Considerations, 12, 23
Contiguous communities, 111
Controversy, 63
Conversation, 41, 106
Cossyah language, 42
Cotton, Henry J., 54
Criticism, 11, 13
Cross-cousin marriage, 92
Cunningham, J.R., 59

Customary exchange, 101

Das Gupta, K., 145
Datta, Birendranath, 101
Democratisation, 69
Descending generation, 96-97,98
Dhekeris, 104
Dialectology, 106
Dibrugarh, 56
Dibrugarh University, 86
Dissimilarities, 117
Distinguishing features, 22
Dualized nationalities, 22
Dutta, Rai Bahadur Pramod
 Chandra, 62

Earle, Sir Archdale, 60
East India Company, 30-31, 35,
 40, 49
Economic exploitation, 31
 frustration, 81
Eden, Ashley, 36
Education, associated words,
 112-13
 missionary policy of, 40
 spread of, 120
Elliot, Charles, 53, 72
Employment, 40
Ethnic groups, 22
Ethnographic background, 91-92
Etymology, 26
European languages, 121
Evangelism, 41
Exogamous, 92
Exploration, 13
Export trade, 40

Fierce marauders, 31
First Khasi Bible, 32
Food habits words, 113-14
Fuller, J.B., policy, 56-57

Gandhiji, 23
Garo, ascending generation of,
 98-99
 language, 24, 73, 89
 nationalities, 22, 24
Garo Kinship, 93
 terminology, 191
Gauhati University, 86
 entrance examination, 57
Geeta, 43
German missionaries, 72
Goalpara, 52-53
 problems in, 58
Goalpara Local Board's Resolu-
 tion, 62
Goddess Kali, 39
Gomastas, 31-32
Goswami, A., 111
Goswami, M.C., 92
Government policy, 51-52, 62
Grammatical forms, 102
 rules, 14
Greeks language, 121
Grierson, G.A., 121
Guha, Amalendu, 15, 21
Gurdon, P.R.T., 59

Haughton, J.C., 43
Hindustani terms, 111
Hoijer, Harry, 89
Huang Ho, 131

Hunter, W.W., 28
Hybrid languages, 109

Illich, Ivan, 14
Immigrant, 60-61
Industrialisation, 106
Inner strength, 122-23
Insensitiveness, 12
Islamic course, 61
    education, 61-62

Jeeban Roy, 44
Jik-Mangma (wife-elephant), 93
Johnson, Luttman, 52
Jorhat, 56, 58
Jorhat Sarbajanik Sabha, 63

Kacharis, 166
Kakati, B., 103
Kamrupi folk songs, 105
Kathagurucharita, 108
Keith, J.J., 74
Khampti, 74, 75
Khashee new Testament, 71
Khasi, 22, 24, 30
    alphabet, 73
    commercial terms, 29
    intellectuals, 45
    loan words in, 29
    population, 28
    religion and culture, 45
    use of script, 29-30
Khasi-Bengali relations, 27, 30
Khasi language,
    affection, 129
    assumptions, 125-26
    causation, 129
    for action, 129
    individual volition, 128
    relation, 128
    subsidiary categories, 126
    techniques, 126
    translation, 126
Khasi Hills Baptist Mission, 34-35
Khasi-Jaintias hills, 26, 28
Khasi nationalism, 23
Khasi renaissance, 43
Khasi Unitarian Mission, 46
Khonglah, Jeep Sandy, 125
Kinship terminology, 90, 92-94, 97-98, 100
Kinship suffixes, 93
Kiratas, 77, 130
Koches, 103
Krishna Pal, 32
Kuki, 76,

Lai-Haraoba festivals, 78
Laimaren deities,78
Languages, 12, 26, 28, 56, 58-60, 73, 84, 89-90, 120, 145-150, 152-155
    controversy, 63
    demand of, 86
    fricatives in, 138
    families of, 130
    games, 14
    learning facilities, 86
    phenomenon of, 11
    politics, 21

problems, 83, 89
sociology of, 117, 124
fear and distrust, 121-22
inner strength, 122-23
standard forms of, 102,
Language situation, approaches, 21-22
Lindsay, Robert, 30, 32
Linguistic affinity, awareness of, 81-82, 118-19
Linguistic identity, 81
Linguistic peculiarities, 90, 130
Linguistic unawareness, 118-19
Lish, Alexander Burgh, 34, 35, 38
Loan words, 115-16
London Baptist Mission, 74
Lord Dalhousie, 42
Lyngdoh, Homiwell, 46

Machang, 95
Madur Maskut, 71
Mahabharatc, 43, 76-77, 130
Maghi language, 120
Mahari, 95
Maithili language, 120
Majumdar, D.N., 89
Mangaldoiya dialect, 104
Manipur,
hills and valleys, 78, 80
language and culture, 76, 80
tribal society of, 80
unemployment, 81
Manipur Chakra, 77
Manipur Cultural Integration Conference, 78
Martin, C.A., 52
Masoi, 30
Melties, 76-77, 79
language, 80
Melitus, P.G., 55
Miju, non-voiced stop in, 51-52
Mills, A.J.M., 42
Missing,
consonant cluster, 139-40
consonant sound, 138-39
gemination in, 139-40
Missing phonology, 135, 144
stops, 136, 38
supra-segmented features, 144
syllabic structure, 143-44
varieties of, 134-35
vowels and diphthongs, 136, 140-41
Mizo alphabat, 74
language, 74-75
Mofussils, 54
Moklum Tongsa, 148
Mongoloid roots, 81
Montague-Chelmsford Reforms, 61, 62
Muhammedans, 103
education conference, 60
Muktab, 61
Multilingual composition, 66-67
Multilingual society, 66, 84
Mutual competition, 23

Naga languages, 22, 24-25, 118, 132
Nagaland, 83-84
population, 83-84
Nalini Natarajan, 3r3

Nata Mandaps,77
Nationalism, 22-23
Nationalities, 21-24
Neoseksari, 99
Nepali language, 123
New complication, 60
New education system, 113
New testament, 33-34, 71, 73-74
Nilkanta Singh, E., 76
Nongkhlaw, 37
Nongkseh, 71
North-Eastern Hill University, 86
Nuclear family, 93-94

Old Testament, 73-74

Paikars, 31, 32
Pali script ,74
Peculiarities, 106,107
People's Liberation Army (PLA), 81
Phani Bora, 64
Polygyny, 92
Polygynous families, 93
Phrase structure, 102
Pragjyotish, 130
Pronunciation, 102, 108
 peculiarities of, 107
Propositions, 89
Pseudo-Vaisnava sect, 107

Rajbansi dialect, 104
Ramakrishna Mission, 46
Ramayana, 43, 130
Rati khowa, 107
Ratnavali, 28
Regional homogeneities, 23
Revivalism, 43-44
Revivalist movement, 46
Robinson, William, 41
Roman script, 41-42
Royal Chronicle, 76

Saadulla, Sayed Muhammed, 62, 63, 64
Sanads, 39
Sanamahi, 78
Sankaradeva, 108
Santali language, 120
Scandalised, 101, 102
Scott, David 27, 36
Secrat restricted language, 107
Serampore Mission, 34, 35, 71
Sexual relation, 92
Shifting cultivation, 78
Siamese language, 70
Sibcharan Roy, 44, 45, 46
Sibsagar, 56, 102
 dialect, 104, 105-106
Sinha, A.P., 125
Sinha, Sarat Chandra, 66
Sino-Tibetan languages, 114, 130-33
 classification, 131-32
Singpho, consonat cluster of, 151-52
Social circumstances, 70
Societies, conglomeration of, 117
Sociolinguistics, 106
Socio-politico-linguistic confusion, 120-21
Sororal polygyny, 92

Spelling pattern, 72-73
Sturtevant, E.H., 102
Superior languages, 120
Surma valley, 27, 57
Sylhet, 65

Taid, Tabu, 134
Talukder, B.N., 83
Text Books hurdle, 52-53
Tibeto-Burman languages, 77, 102, 134
Tibeto-Chinese languages, 123
Tirat Singh,U., 37
Tribes, distribution of, 145
Tribal languages, 107, 108, 117-18, 120-21, 122-24
Trudgill, Peter, 90
Tunga, Sudhansu, S., 15, 115

University syllabus, 56
Upanishada, 43
Urban dialects, 106

Vaishnavism, 78
Vidyasagar, Iswar Chandra, 113
Verbal expression, 148
Vowal harmony, 149-50

Ward, William E., 54, 55
Welsh Alvinist Methodist Mission, 35, 42, 41, 44
Welsh Christian Mission, 70
Welsh Missionaries, 46, 69, 72
Western Assam, principal dialects of, 103-104
White conspiracy, 37
Whorf, Benjamin, 90
William, J., 53, 55
Wittgenstein, 12, 14

Younger siblings, 93

Zamindars, 61
Zeleriangrong (Tamenglong), 78
Zemi-Rongmei Langmei (Kabuis), 78